LSAT Hacks

LSAT Preptest 75 Explanations

A Study Guide for LSAT 75
(June 2015 LSAT)

Graeme Blake

Blake Publications
Montreal, Canada

http://lsathacks.com

ISBN 13: 978-1-927997-10-9
ISBN 10: 1-927997-10-0

Testimonials

Self-study is my preferred way to prep, but I often felt myself missing a few questions each test. Especially for Logic Games, I wanted to see those key inferences which I just couldn't seem to spot on my own. That's where *LSAT Hacks* came in. These solutions have been a tremendous help for my prep, and in training myself to think the way an experienced test taker would.

- Spencer B.

Graeme paraphrases the question in plain terms, and walks through each step in obtaining the right answer in a very logical way. This book uses the same techniques as other guides, but its so much more consistent and concise! By the time you read through all the tests, you've gradually developed your eye for the questions. Using this book is a great way to test your mastery of techniques!

- Sara L.

Graeme's explanations have the most logical and understandable layout I've seen in an LSAT prep book. The explanations are straightforward and easy to understand, to the point where they make you smack your forehead and say 'of course!

- Michelle V.

"Graeme is someone who clearly demonstrates not only LSAT mastery, but the ability to explain it in a compelling manner. This book is an excellent addition to whatever arsenal you're amassing to tackle the LSAT."

- J.Y. Ping, 7Sage LSAT,
www.7Sage.com

I did not go through every single answer but rather used the explanations to see if they could explain why my answer was wrong and the other correct. I thought the breakdown of "Type", "Conclusion", "Reasoning" and "Analysis" was extremely useful in simplifying the question. As for quality of the explanations I'd give them a 10 out of 10.

- Christian F.

LSAT PrepTests come with answer keys, but it isn't sufficient to know whether or not you picked the credited choice to any given question. The key to making significant gains on this test is understanding the logic underlying the questions.

This is where Graeme's explanations really shine. You may wonder whether your reasoning for a specific question is sound. For the particularly challenging questions, you may be at a complete loss as to how they should be approached.

Having these questions explained by Graeme who scored a 177 on the test is akin to hiring an elite tutor at a fraction of the price. These straightforward explanations will help you improve your performance and, more fundamentally, enhance your overall grasp of the test content.

- Morley Tatro, Cambridge LSAT,
www.cambridgelsat.com

Through his conversational tone, helpful introductions, and general recommendations and tips, Graeme Blake has created an enormously helpful companion volume to *The Next Ten Actual Official LSATs*. He strikes a nice balance between providing the clarity and basic explanation of the questions that is needed for a beginner and describing the more complicated techniques that are necessary for a more advanced student.

Even though the subject matter can be quite dry, Graeme succeeds in making his explanations fun and lighthearted. This is crucial: studying for the LSAT is a daunting and arduous task. By injecting some humor and keeping a casual tone, the painful process of mastering the LSAT becomes a little less painful.

When you use *LSAT Hacks* in your studying, you will feel like you have a fun and knowledgeable tutor guiding you along the way.

- Law Schuelke, LSAT Tutor,
www.lawLSAT.com

Graeme's explanations are clear, concise and extremely helpful. They've seriously helped me increase my understanding of the LSAT material!

- Jason H.

Graeme's book brings a different view to demystifying the LSAT. The book not only explains the right and wrong answers, but teaches you how to read the reading comprehension and the logical reasoning questions. His technique to set up the games rule by rule help me not making any fatal mistakes in the set up. The strategies he teaches can be useful for someone starting as much as for someone wanting to perfect his strategies. Without his help my LSAT score would have been average, he brought my understanding of the LSAT and my score to a higher level even if english is not my mother tongue.

- Patrick Du.

This book is a must buy for any who are looking to pass or improve their LSAT, I highly recommend it.

- Patrick Da.

This book was really useful to help me understand the questions that I had more difficulty on. When I was not sure as to why the answer to a certain question was that one, the explanations helped me understand where and why I missed the right answer in the first place. I recommend this book to anyone who would like to better understand the mistakes they make.

- Pamela G.

Graeme's book is filled with thoughtful and helpful suggestions on how to strategize for the LSAT test. It is well-organized and provides concise explanations and is definitely a good companion for LSAT preparation.

- Lydia L.

The explanations are amazing, great job. I can hear your voice in my head as I read through the text.

- Shawn M.

LSAT Hacks, especially the logic games sections, was extremely helpful to my LSAT preparation.

The one downside to self study is that sometimes we do not know why we got a question wrong and thus find it hard to move forward. Graeme's book fixes that; it offers explanations and allows you to see where you went wrong. This is an extremely helpful tool and I'd recommend it to anybody that's looking for an additional study supplement.

- Joseph C.

Regardless of how well you're scoring on the LSAT, this book is very helpful. I used it for LR and RC. It breaks down and analyzes each question without the distraction of classification and complicated methods you'll find in some strategy books. Instead of using step-by-step procedures for each question, the analyses focus on using basic critical thinking skills and common sense that point your intuition in the right direction. Even for questions you're getting right, it still helps reinforce the correct thought process. A must-have companion for reviewing prep tests.

- Christine Y.

Take a thorough mastery of the test, an easygoing demeanor, and a genuine desire to help, and you've got a solid resource for fine-tuning your approach when you're tirelessly plowing through test after test. Written from the perspective of a test-taker, this book should help guide your entire thought process for each question, start to finish.

- Yoni Stratievsky, Harvard Ready, www.harvardready.com

This LSAT guide is the best tool I could have when preparing for the LSAT. Not only does Graeme do a great job of explaining the sections as a whole, he also offers brilliant explanations for each question. He takes the time to explain why an answer is wrong, which is far more helpful when trying to form a studying pattern.

- Amelia F.

LSAT 75 Explanations
Table Of Contents

Introduction

The LSAT is a hard test.

The only people who take the LSAT are smart people who did well in University. The LSAT takes the very best students, and forces them to compete.

If the test's difficulty shocked you, this is why. The LSAT is a test designed to be hard for smart people.

That's the bad news. But there's hope. The LSAT is a *standardized* test. It has patterns. It can be learned.

To get better, you have to review your mistakes. Many students write tests and move on, without fully understanding their mistakes.

This is understandable. The LSAC doesn't publish official explanations for most tests. It's hard to be sure why you were wrong.

That's where this book comes in. It's a companion for LSAT 75, the June 2015 LSAT.

This book lets you see where you went wrong. It has a full walk through of each question and of every answer choice. You can use this book to fix your mistakes, and make sure you understand *everything*.

By getting this book, you've shown that you're serious about beating this test. I sincerely hope it helps you get the score you want.

There are a few things that I'd like to highlight.

Logical Reasoning: It can be hard to identify conclusions in LR. You don't get feedback on whether you identified the conclusion correctly.

This book gives you that feedback. I've identified the conclusion and the reasoning for each argument. Try to find these on your own beforehand, and make sure they match mine.

Logic Games: Do the game on your own before looking at my explanation. You can't think about a game unless you're familiar with the rules. Once you read my explanations, draw my diagrams yourself on a sheet of paper. You'll understand them much better by recopying them.

Reading Comprehension: You should form a mental map of the passage. This helps you locate details quickly. Make a 1-2 line summary of each paragraph (it can be a mental summary).

I've written my own summaries for each passage. They show the minimum amount of information that you should know after reading a passage, without looking back.

I've included line references in my explanations. You do not need to check these each time. They're only there in case you aren't sure where something is.

Do these three things, and you can answer most Reading Comprehension questions with ease.:

1. Know the point of the passage.
2. Understand the passage, in broad terms. Reread anything you don't understand.
3. Know where to find details. That's the point of the paragraph summaries. I usually do mine in my head, and they're shorter than what I've written.

Review This Book

Before we start, I'd like to ask you a favor. I'm an independent LSAT instructor. I don't have a marketing budget.

But I do my best to make good guides to the LSAT. If you agree, I would love it if you took two minutes to write a review on amazon.com

People judge a book by its reviews. So if you like this guide you can help others discover it. I'd be very grateful.

Good luck!

Graeme

p.s. I'm a real person, and I want to know how the LSAT goes and what you think of this book. Send me an email at graeme@lsathacks.com!

p.p.s. For more books, check out the further reading section at the back. I also link to a free five part email course about how to study for the LSAT.

How To Use This Book

The word "Hacks" in the title is meant in the sense used by the tech world and Lifehacker: "solving a problem" or "finding a better way".

The LSAT can be beaten, but you need a good method. My goal is for you to use this book to understand your mistakes and master the LSAT.

This book is *not* a replacement for practicing LSAT questions on your own.

You have to try the questions by yourself first. When you review, try to see why you were wrong *before* you look at my explanations.

Active review will teach you to fix your own mistakes. The explanations are there for when you have difficulty solving on a question on your own or when you want another perspective on a question.

When you *do* use the explanations, have the question on hand. These explanations are not meant to be read alone. You should use them to help you think about the questions more deeply.

Most of the logical reasoning explanations are pretty straightforward. Necessary assumption questions are often an exception, so I want to give you some guidance to help you interpret the explanations.

The easiest way to test the right answer on a necessary assumption question is to "negate" it.

You negate a statement by making it false, in the slightest possible way. For example, the negation of "The Yankees will win all their games" is "The Yankees will *not* win all their games (they will lose at least one)."

You *don't* have to say that the Yankees will lose *every* game. That goes too far.

If the negation of an answer choice proves the conclusion wrong, then that answer is *necessary* to the argument, and it's the correct answer.

Often, I negate the answer choices when explaining necessary assumption questions, so just keep in mind why they're negated.

Logic games also deserve special mention.

Diagramming is a special symbolic language that you have to get comfortable with to succeed.

If you just *look* at my diagrams without making them yourself, you may find it hard to follow along. You can only learn a language by using it yourself.

So you will learn *much* more if you draw the diagrams on your own. Once you've seen how I do a setup, try to do it again by yourself.

With constant practice, you *will* get better at diagramming, and soon it will come naturally.

But you must try on your own. Draw the diagrams.

Note that when you draw your own diagrams, you don't have to copy every detail from mine. For example, I often leave off the numbers when I do linear games. I've included them in the book, because they make it easier for you to follow along.

But under timed conditions, I leave out many details so that I can draw diagrams faster. If you practice making drawings with fewer details, they become just as easy to understand.

Keep diagrams as minimal as possible.

If you simply don't *like* the way I draw a certain rule type, then you can substitute in your own style of diagram. Lots of people succeed using different styles of drawing.

Just make sure your replacement is easy to draw consistently, and that the logical effect is the same. I've chosen these diagrams because they are clear, they're easy to draw, and they *keep you from forgetting rules*.

I've included line references to justify Reading Comprehension Answers. Use these only in case you're unsure about an explanation. You don't have to go back to the passage for every line reference.

Short Guide to Logical Reasoning

LR Question Types

Must be True: The correct answer is true.

Most Strongly Supported: The correct answer is probably true.

Strengthen/Weaken: The answer is correct if it even slightly strengthens/weakens the argument.

Parallel Reasoning: The correct answer will mirror the argument's structure exactly. It is often useful to diagram these questions (but not always).

Sufficient Assumption: The correct answer will prove the conclusion. It's often useful to diagram sufficient assumption questions. For example:

The conclusion is: A → D

There is a gap between premises and conclusion:

A   B → C → D   **missing link:** A → B or B̶ → A̶

A → B → C   D   **missing link:** C → D or D̶ → C̶

A → B   C → D   **missing link:** B → C or C̶ → B̶

The right answer will provide the missing link.

Necessary Assumption: The correct answer will be essential to the argument's conclusion. Use the negation technique: If the correct answer is false (negated), then the argument falls apart.
The negation of hot is "not hot" rather than cold.

Here's how to do negations: You just make the idea false. This is not so much about grammar as it is about thinking what the idea is, and a counterexample. E.g.

"All Americans are nice" → "One guy in Arkansas named Bob is sort of mean. Every single other American is always really nice"

The "grammatical" negation is "not all Americans are nice", but it's so much clearer and easier to think in terms of making the idea not true.

Important: Try to make the answer false but *not* hurt the argument. This will eliminate wrong answers. The correct answer will *always* destroy the argument if negated. If you can correctly negate an answer but imagine a situation where the argument is still fine, then that's not the right answer.

Point at Issue: Point at Issue questions require two things. **1.** The two speakers must express an opinion on something. **2.** They must disagree about it.

Flawed Reasoning: The correct answer will be a description of a reasoning error made in the argument. It will often be worded very abstractly.

Practice understanding the answers, right and wrong. Flawed Reasoning answers are very abstract, but they all mean something. Think of examples to make them concrete and easier to understand.

Basic Logic

Take the phrase: "All cats have tails."

"Cats" is the sufficient condition. Knowing that something is a cat is "sufficient" for us to say that it has a tail. "Tails" is a necessary condition, because you can't be a cat without a tail. You can draw this sentence as C → T

The **contrapositive** is a correct logical deduction, and reads "anything without a tail is not a cat." You can draw this as T̶ → C̶. Notice that the terms are reversed, and negated.

Incorrect Reversal: "Anything with a tail is a cat." This is a common logical error on the LSAT.

T → C   (Wrong! Dogs have tails and aren't cats.)

Incorrect Negation: "If it is not a cat, it doesn't have a tail." This is another common error.

C̶ → T̶ (Wrong! Dogs aren't cats, but have tails.)

General Advice: Always remember what you are looking for on each question. The correct answer on a strengthen question would be incorrect on a weaken question.

Watch out for subtle shifts in emphasis between the stimulus and the incorrect answer choices. An example would be the difference between "how things are" and "how things should be."

Justify your answers. If you're tempted to choose an answer choice that says something like the sentence below, then be sure you can fill in the blank:

Answer Choice Says: "The politician attacked his opponents' characters",

Fill In The Blank: "The politician said _____ about his opponents' characters."

If you cannot say what the attack was, you can't pick that answer. This applies to many things. You must be able to show that the stimulus supports your idea.

A Few Logic Games Tips

Rule 1: When following along with my explanations....draw the diagrams yourself, too!

This book will be much more useful if you try the games by yourself first. You must think through games on your own, and no book will do that for you. You must have your mind in a game to solve it.

Use the explanations when you find a game you can't understand on your own, or when you want to know how to solve a game more efficiently.

Some of the solutions may seem impossible to get on your own. It's a matter of practice. When you learn how to solve one game efficiently, solving other games becomes easier too.

Try to do the following when you solve games:

Work With What Is Definite: Focus on what must be true. Don't figure out every possibility.

Draw Your Deductions: Unsuccessful students often make the same deductions as successful students. But the unsuccessful students forget their deductions, 15 seconds later! I watch this happen.

Draw your deductions, or you'll forget them. Don't be arrogant and think this doesn't happen to you. It would happen to *me* if I didn't draw my deductions.

Draw Clear Diagrams: Many students waste time looking back and forth between confusing pictures. They've done everything right, but can't figure out their own drawings!

You should be able to figure out your drawings 3 weeks later. If you can't, then they aren't clear enough. I'm serious: look back at your old drawings. Can you understand them? If not, you need a more consistent, cleaner system.

Draw Local Rules: When a question gives you a new rule (a local rule), draw it. Then look for deductions by combining the new rule with your existing rules. Then double-check what you're being asked and see if your deduction is the right answer. This works 90% of the time for local rule questions. And it's fast.

If you don't think you have time to draw diagrams for each question, practice drawing them faster. It's a learnable skill, and it pays off.

Try To Eliminate a Few Easy Answer Choices First: You'll see examples in the explanations that show how certain deductions will quickly get rid of 1-3 answer choices on many questions. This saves time for harder answer choices and it frees up mental space.

You don't have to try the answer choices in order, without thinking about them first.

Split Games Into Two Scenarios When Appropriate: If a rule only allows something to be one of two ways (e.g. F is in 1 or 7), then draw two diagrams: one with F in 1, and one with F in 7. This leads to extra deductions surprisingly often. And it always makes the game easier to visualize.

Combine Rules To Make Deductions: Look for variables that appear in multiple rules. These can often be combined. Sometimes there are no deductions, but it's a crime not to look for them.

Reread The Rules: Once you've made your diagram, reread the rules. This lets you catch any mistakes, which are fatal. It doesn't take very long, and it helps you get more familiar with the rules.

Draw Rules Directly On The Diagram: Mental space is limited. Three rules are much harder to remember than two. When possible, draw rules on the diagram so you don't have to remember them.

Memorize Your Rules: You should memorize every rule you can't draw on the diagram. It doesn't take long, you'll go faster, and you'll make fewer mistakes. Try it, it's not that hard.

If you spend 30 seconds doing this, you'll often save a minute by going through the game faster.

You should also make a numbered list of rules that aren't on the diagram, in case you need to check them.
A.

Section I – Logical Reasoning

Question 1

QUESTION TYPE: Necessary Assumption

CONCLUSION: The city could have earned extra money by raising parking fees, if it hadn't sold the rights to the fees.

REASONING: The city sold parking fee rights to a private company. The company raised rates and is earning more money.

ANALYSIS: The pundit's argument makes a false equivalence between the city and the private company. There are differences between a company and a local government. It's possible that the city would not have been able to raise fees.

- Maybe the company is more competent.
- Maybe the city would face public pressure if it raised fees.
- Maybe the city leaders would have been too reluctant to raise fees.

Etc. There are always alternate possibilities, and the pundit failed to establish that the city could have successfully raised rates.

————————

A. The pundit is talking about what would happen if the city *didn't* sell the rights to a private company. So it doesn't matter if any other companies are available – the city isn't selling!
B. CORRECT. If the city couldn't have raised fees, then the pundit is wrong to say the city could have earned more money.
    Negation: The city couldn't have raised rates, had they kept the rights to them.
C. This tells us what the city *should* do. But the argument is about what the city *could* do. Those aren't the same thing.
D. It doesn't matter what factors the city needs to consider in setting rates. This argument is about a yes or no question: *could* the city have raised rates, or not?
E. This *weakens* the argument if true. It provides a reason the city *couldn't* earn as much money as the private company did.

Question 2

QUESTION TYPE: Principle – Justify

CONCLUSION: Popular science publications shouldn't try to explain new scientific developments to a large audience.

REASONING: Writing that explains new scientific developments will either be wrong (due to metaphors) or it won't reach a large audience (because it's rigorous).

ANALYSIS: The author is saying that popular science shouldn't try to reach a wide audience, because popular science authors have to use (often inaccurate) metaphors to do that.

So what? To prove the argument, the author should have said "we *should not* describe science in an inaccurate way" or something like that.

On principle questions there is generally a gap between what *is* true and what *should* be true.

————————

A. The author is saying we should avoid the kind of writing that uses metaphors. "Balancing" metaphors doesn't fit with the argument.
B. This just tells us a fact about scientific arguments. We don't need a fact. We need a principle that tells us what we *should* do.
C. CORRECT. This principle lets us decide what to do. We know that reaching a wide audience forces us to use inaccurate metaphors. Therefore this answer tells us that it's better to be accurate even if we can't reach a wide audience.
D. This principle tells us the *opposite* of what we're looking for. The argument said that we *should not* try to reach a wide audience.
E. This answer just tells us a fact. We're looking for a principle that tells us what we *should* do. Further, it doesn't matter if even rigorous writing must have some metaphors. It only matters if rigorous writing has fewer and more accurate metaphors than writing meant for a wide audience.

Question 3

QUESTION TYPE: Necessary Assumption

CONCLUSION: Rock music is all bad.

REASONING: We already knew that rock music has no moral worth and destroys society. But at least old rock LPs had nice art. But now digital music means people don't buy many LPs.

ANALYSIS: This is a bad argument. It tells us that one advantage is gone (LP sales are ending). But it introduces a new factor, digital music, and doesn't tell us whether digital music gives rock some redeeming value.

_____

A. CORRECT. If digital music has nice art, then maybe rock music still has some value.
Negation: Digital music is distributed with innovative art.

B. The argument is *stronger* if this is false. We're looking for something that helps the argument if it's true, not something that hurts it.
Negation: Few of the small number of LPs produced today are rock LPs.

C. This answer is helpful, but it's not necessary. The negation of this answer doesn't affect the argument.
Negation: In the 1960s and 70s, almost all of the nice LP art was on rock albums. But one jazz album also had innovative art.

D. It's helpful to know that LPs still have innovative art. But this doesn't matter. The point of the argument is that few LPs are being produced today.

E. This *weakens* the argument. It says rock music is even worse than it used to be. Necessary assumption answers are supposed to strengthen the argument if true (and destroy it if false).

Question 4

QUESTION TYPE: Method of Reasoning

CONCLUSION: Babbling is linguistic.

REASONING: Babies open their mouths wider on the right when they babble. Earlier studies have shown that people open their mouths wider on the left when they're making non-linguistic sounds.

ANALYSIS: The scientist asks whether baby babbling is linguistic or not. Then they present two points of evidence to show that babbling is linguistic.

Simple as that. I had trouble with this question because I was overthinking it. E describes a very standard argument: ask a question and prove one side. Not every argument has to be complex.

There's no way to "explain" why the wrong answers are wrong. They just don't match. So I'm providing an example of what that type of argument looks like.

_____

A. There's no counterargument. The author only argues their point directly.
Example of method: It may seem that babies have meaning when they babble, because they are expressive. But actually studies have shown expression can occur without any meaning.

B. This is totally different.
Example of method: Some say we should live in central areas. But if everyone did that, central areas fill up. We should live in areas with low rents.

C. This is different.
Example of method: Do babies have meaning when they babble? We could test this by using the experimental Dapler method. In fact this method is necessary since all other methods have failed to produce results.

D. This is a completely different argument.
Example of method: How did the car get on the roof? Maybe people lifted it up using a crane. But no one saw a crane. However, there are some crane tracks nearby, so it likely was the crane.

E. CORRECT. This matches exactly. The two interpretations are: babbling is linguistic, or babbling is *not* linguistic. The studies provide evidence that babbling is linguistic.

Question 5

QUESTION TYPE: Weaken

CONCLUSION: Planting trees will help us meet our commitment to reducing carbon dioxide (CO_2) emissions.

REASONING: Trees absorb carbon dioxide (CO_2).

ANALYSIS: This seems like a good argument. But it's a weaken question, so there must be something wrong with it.

I couldn't prephrase anything here. I just went into the answers knowing I was looking for something that explained why trees wouldn't reduce CO_2 emissions even though they absorb CO_2.

Note the difference between *emissions* and *absorption*. The right answer shows tree planting causes more emissions. That's not contradicting the idea that trees also absorb CO_2.

––––––––––––––

A. This describes a difficulty in planting trees. But the environment minister wasn't arguing that it would be easy to plant trees.
Instead, they're talking about what would happen *if* we plant a large number of trees.
B. Who the hell cares whether the proportion of deforested land has increased faster or slower than CO_2 emissions?
This is an irrelevant comparison. There are very few cases where an answer like this is right. They're mostly nonsense.
C. CORRECT. This shows that, in the short term, planting trees releases more CO_2 than it absorbs.
D. It might be nice to reduce emissions faster, but that's irrelevant to the conclusion. The environment minister is making a factual argument: what will happen *if* we plant trees?
E. The minister wasn't talking about other gases. They didn't claim that trees planting is a complete solution to global warming. They only made the very limited claim that planting trees will reduce CO_2 emissions.

Question 6

QUESTION TYPE: Paradox

PARADOX: SUVs are safer for those riding in them, but auto safety experts say that the increase in SUV ownership is cause for worry.

ANALYSIS: In any car crash, there are *two* cars involved. And the argument only said that SUVs are safer for those *in* the SUV.

So the traffic fatality statistics could show that SUVs are safer for those in them but more dangerous for those in the other car.

––––––––––––––

A. This increases the paradox. Assuming that people know SUVs are safer, this would cause people to be better at driving them. We're looking for a reason that SUVs are *dangerous*.
B. Fuel tank capacity isn't relevant to safety. You might be thinking that a large fuel tank could cause larger explosions....but that's a huge stretch.
Answers suck – don't work so hard to prove them right.
C. This seems very tempting. If vehicles carry more people, then there are more people that could die in accidents.
Careful. This answer *did not* say that SUVs lead to more people on the road. It's possible that there are more people in SUVs, but fewer vehicles on the road. I.e. people could all drive in one SUV instead of two smaller cars.
So there'd be the same number of people driving, and no greater risk.
It's also possible that people are switching from other large vehicles (such as vans) to SUVs. So there'd be no change in average passenger distribution.
In any case, it is not a reasonable assumption that a high average number of people in SUVs leads to more people on the road.
D. CORRECT. This shows that SUVs may be safer for those in them, but also more likely to cause damage to people in other cars.
E. This has no impact. If SUVs are as likely to be involved in accidents, then that *eliminates* a possible difference. We want to show a difference!

Question 7

QUESTION TYPE: Flawed Reasoning

CONCLUSION: Sherwood supports higher taxes.

REASONING: Sherwood was on city council when city council raised taxes.

ANALYSIS: This is a silly argument. The political advertisement ignores an obvious possibility: Sherwood could have voted *against* the tax increases.

This is a part-to-whole flaw. You can be part of something without sharing all of its properties.

A. Nonsense. There's no limited sample. The advertisement was considering the council as a whole.
   Example of flaw: Americans are all named Bob. I say this because my Uncle Bob is an American, and he's named Bob.
B. This is a different flaw.
   Example of flaw: Death must be a good thing, because death is inevitable.
C. This is a different flaw.
   Example of flaw: If Sherwood wins 100% of the votes, he will be elected. So if Sherwood only wins 95% of the votes, he will lose.
D. This describes an ad hominem flaw. That didn't happen.
   Example of flaw: Sherwood smells bad. Don't vote for him.
E. **CORRECT.** The "whole" is city council. It voted for taxes. Sherwood is an individual. He might have voted against taxes. The vote might have passed 13-6, for example.

Question 8

QUESTION TYPE: Identify the Conclusion

CONCLUSION: The catering company shouldn't raise their rates.

REASONING: The catering company's mission is to provide low-cost gourmet catering.

ANALYSIS: There are two major clues that indicate the conclusion here:

- The word "should". A sentence with the word "should" tends to be the conclusion.
- "After all". This indicates that the sentence is evidence that supports the previous sentence.

Both of these tell us that the third sentence is the conclusion: the gourmet catering company shouldn't raise rates.

The sentence about the company training and hiring new staff isn't structurally relevant to the argument. It's just context explaining why the catering company is raising rates.

A. This is just a fact. The client is arguing that the catering company should reconsider.
B. This is just the reason that the catering company wants to raise rates. The client's conclusion is that the catering company should reconsider that decision.
C. **CORRECT.** See the analysis above.
   You might have hesitated to choose this answer since it didn't mention reconsidering.
   But since the conclusion said "reconsider *and* not raise their rates." It's implied that the author will only be happy if the reconsideration results in not changing rates.
D. This is just a fact supporting the conclusion. *Because* the company mission is to provide low-cost catering, the client argues the company shouldn't raise rates.
E. This is a fact supporting the conclusion that the catering company therefore shouldn't raise its rates.

Question 9

QUESTION TYPE: Strengthen

CONCLUSION: The red admiral butterfly's irregular flight style evolved to help the butterfly avoid enemies.

REASONING: Predators will eat nonpoisonous butterflies like the red admiral. Predators avoid poisonous butterflies.

ANALYSIS: This sounds like a good argument. But the author ignores the possibility that *all* butterflies have an irregular flight style, and that red admirals use some other defense to avoid predators.

I mean, have you ever looked at a butterfly? Those things fly all over the place. We need more information about butterfly flight styles.

_____

A. **CORRECT.** Poisonous butterflies don't need to avoid predators. If none of them have flight styles similar to the red admiral's, then that strengthens the idea that the red admiral developed this flight style because *because* red admirals aren't poisonous.
B. Who cares? Being crushed by a car is not the most common cause of death for humans, but you still take precautions against getting crushed by cars, right?
It almost never matters what the most common or most important cause of something is.
C. It's hard to say what effect this has. If other non-poisonous butterflies share the flight style, then that helps the argument.
But if poisonous butterflies share the flight style, then that *hurts* the argument.
This answer doesn't say which other butterflies share the flight style.
D. Who cares about other, heavier insects. I imagine that *anything* a small insect like a butterfly does is more energy efficient than what a large insect does.
I mean, humans are more energy efficient in their movements than elephants, but that doesn't tell us much about human or elephant behavior.
E. This provides zero information. We know nothing about how those other non-poisonous butterflies avoid predators.

Question 10

QUESTION TYPE: Principle – Strengthen

CONCLUSION: Providing copyright protection several decades past author lifetime is too much.

REASONING: Some copyright is justified. Copyright helps society by incentivizing creative works. But copyright hurts society by creating protected monopolies. The additional benefit of longer copyright is outweighed by the cost of longer copyright.

ANALYSIS: This already seems like a good argument. That's because the LSAT makes a strict separation between fact and morals. If I say "the building is burning down, we should leave" then you likely agree with me. But that's because you are already adding an extra moral principle "I *should* not stay in a burning building".

On "principle-justify" questions, the right answer explicitly states the principle that already seems obvious. The principle will be something like "We shouldn't do things that have a net cost to society."

_____

A. This doesn't match the situation.
Example of situation that matches: This copyright statute does help authors. But it seems like it hurts authors. Therefore authors don't like it. We should change the statute's wording.
B. The argument is talking in the present tense. There has been no change in conditions.
(A change in conditions is something in the past like "in the past we rode horses, now we drive cars".)
C. So? This would only let us conclude "Some sort of copyright statute is justified in every country."
D. This principle adds a necessary condition. Copyright statutes enhance rights to creative works, so they already meet this necessary condition. Therefore this principle has no impact.
E. **CORRECT.** Copyright statutes *are* justified due to their benefit to society (see the first sentence). So this tells us that extending copyright decades after author death is a bad thing to do, because that has costs that exceed benefits.

Question 11

QUESTION TYPE: Weaken

CONCLUSION: The police chief says her strategy caused the 20% drop in crime.

REASONING: A 20% drop in crime occurred while the chief was using her strategy.

ANALYSIS: The chief has made an extremely weak argument. They've only shown a correlation: Their strategy happened at the same time the drop in crime happened.

But we don't know what would have happened *without* the strategy. Maybe crime would have fallen by the same amount or even further.

Note that the final bit of the argument is useless fluff. The information about real-time crime data and focussing police resources is merely context that explains what the chief's strategy was. The argument would be exactly as strong if the chief had said "my strategy of making police wear funny hats."

A. The total amount of crime doesn't matter. Only the *direction* matters. If a chief takes over a dangerous city, it's reasonable to expect the crime rate to remain *high* even if the chief succeeding in *lowering* the crime rate.

B. So? It's normal for crime rates to change a lot over a long period of time. We only care about the change in crime *since* the chief took over. (Ok, if the chief took over in an unusually high year, that would be relevant. But crime rates decades ago are too far back to matter to the chief's record.)

C. So? A decline is still a decline. And the fact that crime didn't rise again shows that the chief's results had staying power!

D. **CORRECT.** This destroys the chief's argument. The chief's strategy doesn't look so great now that we know that the rest of the country experienced an even greater decline. (Presumably with no special strategy.)

E. It doesn't matter about different areas of the city. The chief's argument only refers to the city as a whole.

Question 12

QUESTION TYPE: Flawed Reasoning

CONCLUSION: The governments of Acredia need to care about the people to be successful.

REASONING: Every time the government has fallen, it's been true that the rulers have disregarded the people's needs.

ANALYSIS: This argument only shows a correlation. We don't know if the lack of care towards the people *caused* governments to fall.

Heck, maybe *every* government of Acredia failed to care for the people's needs, even successful governments. Some other factor like war or natural disaster could be the actual cause of government failure.

A. So? The commentator didn't say that governments need to do exactly the same things for the people at all times. It only matters whether governments care.

B. This isn't a flaw! This answer says that absence of a condition "led" to failure. That shows the absence actually *caused* the failure. Therefore the inference is reasonable.
   In the argument the commentator failed to establish that lack of care for the people actually caused failure.

C. This would be a flaw. But we have no reason to expect the Duke of Acredia was biased or unreliable. We know nothing about the Duke. Also, the Duke was only mentioned to add color to the argument. The real evidence is the past history of government failure in Acredia. There was no bias there.

D. **CORRECT.** This is the real problem. The author has only shown that lack of care for the people is *correlated* with failure. They've never shown that lack of care actually *caused* failure.

E. The commentator isn't making an argument about virtue. The *Duke* said virtue is necessary, but the commentator's argument is only about caring for the people's welfare. (Which could be self-interested, not virtuous.)
   So whether we can assess past virtue isn't relevant to the commentator's argument.

Question 13

QUESTION TYPE: Most Strongly Supported

FACTS:

1. Professor Burns made observations of an area where a comet reservoir was claimed to appear.
2. Burns didn't see the comet reservoir.
3. The observations happened in poor conditions.
4. Burns claims that her observations are enough to disprove the earlier sighting.

ANALYSIS: This question tests your understanding of how proof works. And it depends on common sense.

You *know* that poor conditions reduce the reliability of astronomical sightings. That's common sense. You also know that poor conditions don't necessarily make an observation worthless.

That's about all we can say. Professor Burns' observations don't prove there's no comet reservoir. But they at least tell us that it might not be visible in all conditions.

A lot of the wrong answers are based on incorrect logic about what we can prove and what we can't.

A. This doesn't follow. Maybe the reservoir is very hard to spot. We might need more observations or better equipment to know for sure.
B. Nonsense. The poor conditions reduce the reliability of Professor Burns' evidence, to be sure. But there's no way that *absence* of a sighting can be interpreted as support for existence.
C. **CORRECT.** This is the best answer. Professor Burns claimed that her observations disproved the earlier sighting. But the poor conditions show that her observations are not as conclusive as she thinks.
D. Hard to say. If the comet reservoir was supposedly easy to see, then a single failure to observe it in good conditions might be enough to disprove its existence.
E. This is too strong. The recent observations either tell us "the comet reservoir may not be visible under all conditions", and they slightly support the idea that it doesn't exist.

Question 14

QUESTION TYPE: Role in Argument

CONCLUSION: The government shouldn't pass laws requiring politeness.

REASONING: Politeness is good, but enforcing politeness laws would cause more problems than impoliteness does now.

ANALYSIS: This question is asking about the role played by the second sentence. That sentence starts with "but". That's the argument's conclusion: society would be worse if there were politeness laws.

"But" often introduces a conclusion. The word shows that the author disagrees with the first sentence, and it presents the second sentence as their opinion.

The third sentence shows a reason why society wouldn't be better off with politeness laws. This supports the second sentence.

It's not possible to "explain" a lot of the wrong answers. They simply fail to correspond to the argument. Instead I've given examples of what an argument matching those answers would look like.

A. **CORRECT.** See the analysis above. The word "but" in this case indicates that the second sentence is the conclusion.
B. The argument doesn't generalize. An example of a generalization: "Americans tend to be polite."
C. If this answer were true, the sentence in question would be support for an intermediate conclusion. There isn't even an intermediate conclusion in the argument.
D. There isn't a generalization in the argument.
   Example of answer: Americans are extremely nice. For instance I once visited America and a family I didn't know invited me for dinner.
   (The second sentence is the illustration)
E. This didn't happen at all.
   Example of answer: Americans are incredibly polite. They always say please and thank you and are never rude. I conclude that this is due to the vast openness of the country.
   (The second sentence is the one describing a phenomenon.)

Question 15

QUESTION TYPE: Strengthen

CONCLUSION: Some planets with oval orbits around a distant star probably developed those orbits as a results of a encounter with other planets orbiting the same stars.

REASONING: Some comets orbiting our sun had encounters with planets and fell into oval orbits.

ANALYSIS: The author is saying that encounters with planets caused the oval orbits. I couldn't prephrase anything here. So I just went into the answers remembering "they are saying that two planets had an encounter, leading to oval orbits."

If you are *precise* about what you know, you can spot the right answer more easily. That phrasing above let me find the answer quickly.

A couple other notes:

- The fact that some planets around our sun have circular orbits isn't too relevant. All it shows is that not all planets have oval orbits.
- The author didn't say that *every* encounter causes oval orbits. They just said that encounters *could* cause oval orbits.

Not every cause is a 100% sufficient cause that works every time. So an encounter + no oval orbit isn't evidence against the argument.

Note also that the argument is not saying that *only* encounters with other planets can cause oval orbits. The author just says "some of the planets" were, which leaves open the possibility that there are other causes.

A. Who cares which planet is affected more? The argument only requires that it's possible for one planet to affect another planet enough that it takes an oval orbit.
B. So? The author didn't say that planetary encounters *always* produce oval orbits. A close encounter in the solar system + lack of an oval orbit wouldn't harm the argument.

Also the argument didn't say that all planets in the solar system have circular orbits. It just said several do. So if there are oval planets in the solar system too then this answer has even less impact.
C. **CORRECT.** The author said that planetary collisions cause some oval orbits. To have a collision, you need more than one planet. So this answer strengthens the argument by showing that collisions were indeed possible.
D. Careful. This might have been right if it said "a close encounter with *a planet*". But it doesn't say that. It says "with some other object". Those other objects might not be planets.
This answer is too vague to impact the argument.
E. This *weakens* the argument. The author is trying to argue that a collision with another planet caused the oval orbits of planets. Another planet *is* "an other object large enough to affect the planet's orbit."
So the argument *requires* there to be other objects large enough to affect orbits (i.e. other planets).

Question 16

QUESTION TYPE: Role in Argument

CONCLUSION: Seawater irrigated farming would be cheaper than most other irrigated agriculture

REASONING: The largest cost in irrigation is the pumping distance of the water. Seawater wouldn't have to be pumped far. Some agriculture crops can grow with seawater.

ANALYSIS: The question is asking why the author mentions the low cost of pumping seawater.

Well, the conclusion is that seawater irrigation is cheap. The fact that pumping is the greatest cost supports that conclusion, when combined with the fact that seawater isn't expensive to pump.

Don't make questions more complicated than they are. This one is as simple as that.

———————

A. Ridiculous. The argument doesn't disprove any claims!
   Example of argument: Some people say that pumping seawater is cheap. But actually that's only in the short term. In the long run seawater corrodes pipes, leading to very high piping costs.
B. Nonsense. The author isn't arguing against any hypothesis.
   Example of argument: I believe that Jenkins committed the robbery. Some say he was out of the country at the time. This would, if true, undermine my hypothesis. But I know for a fact that Jenkins has no passport, so this alibi must be false.
C. **CORRECT.** Simple as that. The importance of pumping + the low cost of pumping seawater supports the idea that seawater irrigation is cheap.
D. No, the conclusion is that seawater irrigation is cheap. The importance of pumping + the low cost of pumping seawater supports that.
E. The author does not provide any evidence that the greatest expense in irrigation is pumping water.

Question 17

QUESTION TYPE: Most Strongly Supported

FACTS:
1. Everyone has direct experience of the economy.
2. If people have direct experience, they don't defer to journalists.
3. Some critics worry that pessimistic economic journalism will affect people's perception of the economy.
4. Journalists say they can't worry about the effects of their work.

ANALYSIS: I rearranged the facts to make the deduction more obvious. Facts 1 and 2 combine to show that it's unlikely that people will be influenced by journalism about the economy.

———————

A. This is a trap answer. It would have been right if it had said "by the extent of negative reporting" or something like that.
   But it says "by the extent of people's confidence in it"
B. Careful. The stimulus said that people *only* defer to journalists when they lack direct experience. But the stimulus did not say that people *always* defer to journalists when they lack experience. Lack of experience is a necessary condition, but not a sufficient condition.
C. The stimulus supports *the opposite* of this.
D. **CORRECT.** This seems probable. People have direct experience of the economy, so they won't defer to journalists.
E. This isn't supported. We know people don't *defer* to journalists if they have direct experience, but journalists could still be harming people in some other way.
   Journalists *say* they can't worry about the effects of their work, but that doesn't mean they're *right* not to worry.

Question 18

QUESTION TYPE: Flawed Reasoning

CONCLUSION: There is no graft in my department.

REASONING: I know that one form of graft doesn't exist. (Gifts over $100)

ANALYSIS: Your instinct may have been to think that the police captain is wrong about the lack of gifts. But that would be too obvious, and it's not a typical type of LSAT flaw. Answers almost never contract the author.

The real flaw is that the police chief described *one* type of graft: gifts over $100.

But "graft" is a broad term. The definition is:

"practices, esp. bribery, used to secure illicit gains in politics or business; corruption"

You could, for example, accept a job later in return for corrupt services now. That's a form of graft, and it wouldn't fall under the $100 gift definition.

———————————

A. A limited sample would be something like "I asked Bob and Jane and they hadn't taken gifts". The police captain was talking about *her entire precinct,* so the sample is 100% of the precinct.
B. **CORRECT.** If there are other types of graft, then it's possible there's graft in the precinct even if the captain is right about the lack of gifts.
C. This isn't a flaw, and it didn't happen in the argument.
   Example of this: They claim that Jill robbed the bank. This seems probable, since Jill has always talked about how banks are bad and how she wants money. Jill has a history of robbery.
D. This didn't happen.
   Example of flaw: We've proven there's no graft. Therefore, no one in the department has ever done any other bad thing.
E. This almost never happens. It takes gross stupidity to contradict your own argument.
   Example of flaw: I bribed one of my officers to spy on the department to see if there was corruption. He reported no one took bribes. So there are no bribes in my department.

Question 19

QUESTION TYPE: Paradox

PARADOX: In all regions, the average hourly wage went up. In the country, the average hourly wage went down.

ANALYSIS: Sometimes, I see how to solve the paradox, and I prephrase the right answer. In this case, however, I couldn't see how to solve the paradox.

When that happens, the key is to load the two facts into your brain, and see which answer can explain *both* of them:

- Average wages are up in each region.
- Average wages in the country went down.

———————————

A. This just tells us about past history. It says the national trends has been continuing. So? This tells us nothing about regions.
B. **CORRECT.** This solves it. Imagine that there are two regions: povertyland, and mansionland. There are 100 people working in each area. The average wage in povertyland is 10, in mansionland, 50.
   Now imagine that employers move 99 jobs from mansionland to povertyland. Now if jobs in povertyland pay 15, then that will be a raise for the former workers of povertyland, but a large pay cut for the mansionland workers who had to move to povertyland.
   If we also imagine that the one remaining worker in mansionland now earns 60, then it's true that in both regions the average wage is higher, but it's also true that the average wage in the country as a whole is lower.
C. Unemployment is irrelevant. We care about the average wage, not how many people have jobs. (No, you can't assume that unemployment affects average wages)
D. So? This doesn't explain anything. It's normal for there to be different rates of change in different regions.
E. So? It doesn't matter how wages in different industries change. We only care about the overall change of *all* wages.

Question 20

QUESTION TYPE: Most Strongly Supported

FACTS:

1. 35% of deceased schizophrenics in the sample had damage to the subplate.
2. None of the non-schizophrenics in the sample had damage to the subplate.
3. This damage must have occurred before the second fetal trimester.

ANALYSIS: The second fetal trimester is *before* a person is born. The LSAT assumes you have this basic knowledge of anatomy.

So we can say that it seems probable that some people get schizophrenia before birth.

————————————

A. This mixes up the groups involved. The stimulus said that 35% *of schizophrenics* had damaged subplates.
   It's possible that *100% of people with damaged subplates* will have schizophrenia.
   This answer is like saying "10% of undergrads will go on to study law. So 10% of people who study law will have been undergrads once."
B. Hard to say. It's possible that the damaged subplate causes some other damage elsewhere, and it's *that* damage that causes schizophrenia.
C. This is an *extremely* tempting answer, but it's 100% wrong. The stimulus said that the damage to the subplate occurred *prior* to the second fetal trimester. This answer says *after* the second fetal trimester.
   This answer shows why you should read all the answers. E, the correct answer, sounds very similar to this. If you read all the answers, you'd see that both C and E can't be right.
D. This is not supported. We don't know *why* the subplate is damaged before the second trimester. It's possible that some non-genetic harm to the mother (stress, injury, loss of nutrients) causes subplate damage.
E. **CORRECT.** This is supported. The fact that *no* people without schizophrenia had subplate damage is telling.
   Nothing is certain, which is why this answer appropriately says "may".

Question 21

QUESTION TYPE: Strengthen

CONCLUSION: Ranchers will probably buy the device.

REASONING: The device makes noises in cows' ears when they leave pasture, causing them to turn around. Buying the devices for an entire herd would be much more expensive than using fencing.

ANALYSIS: The device offers the same benefits as fences, but it costs more to outfit the entire herd. So there are only three reasons that ranchers would buy devices at current prices:

- Ranchers don't mind paying more for no benefit.
- Ranchers are idiots.
- The entire cow herd doesn't have to be outfitted with the devices.

The first two are not very good explanations. The third one I prephrased. How do you prephrase answers? Put yourself in the shoes of the ranchers. Assume you're not an idiot. What might make you buy the device, even though outfitting your entire herd would be too expensive?

————————————

A. This is irrelevant. The device makers are saying that ranchers will buy *now*, at current prices.
B. **CORRECT.** If this is true, then ranchers wouldn't have to outfit their entire herd with the devices. They could just outfit a few cattle leaders with the devices.
   So devices could be cheaper than fences.
C. This is good. If this weren't true, the argument would be weaker. But this doesn't *strengthen* the argument. We have no evidence that fences are a major cause of stress, so this doesn't show that devices have an advantage.
D. Like C, this doesn't offer an *advantage* for the devices. It merely places them on the same playing field as fences.
E. This is a bit of a trick answer. The stimulus says that outfitting an entire herd is too expensive. "The cost of outfitting an entire herd" would include any bulk discounts. Just like "the cost of buying ten subway passes" includes any discount you'd get for buying 10 or more passes.

Question 22

QUESTION TYPE: Flawed Parallel Reasoning

CONCLUSION: Food co-ops are cheaper than supermarkets.

REASONING: Food co-ops are a type of co-op. Co-ops tend to be cheaper than other stores.

ANALYSIS: This question makes a sort of whole-to-part flaw. It applies a tendency to every individual within a group.

On the whole, consumer co-ops are cheaper. But that doesn't mean that every type of co-op is cheaper. It's possible that *food* co-ops are more expensive on average.

_____

A. This actually is a correct argument, assuming that people who own sports cars drive about as much as others, on average. More gasoline per miles * same number of miles = more gas usage.
B. This is a different flaw. It ignores an obvious reason people might prefer fresh vegetables: they taste better.
C. **CORRECT.** This matches. Public transit, on average, causes less pollution than private transport. But, a bus will cause *some* pollution, whereas a bicycle essentially causes none.
So even though bicycles are private transport, they don't share the average quality of private transport.
D. This is a different flaw. We could correctly conclude that people are *eating* more healthful food than before. The flaw here is assuming that any extra purchases of healthful food will automatically happen at health food stores.
E. This is a different flaw. It's like saying "The best way to avoid being drunk is to drink lots of beer, because beer has less alcohol than vodka and alcohol causes drunkenness".
It's stupid reasoning but it fails to match the stimulus.

Question 23

QUESTION TYPE: Sufficient Assumption

CONCLUSION: It's wrong to say that accidents at railroad crossings are the fault of railroad companies.

REASONING: The gates in front of the crossing warn drivers not to cross, but it's possible to drive around the gates. Drivers are adults who should know better.

ANALYSIS: This question doesn't use conditionals. For all it's wordiness, it really only gives us a single fact that supports the conclusion: adults should know better. We can fill the gap by making a conditional statement between the fact and the conclusion.

Evidence: Adults should know better
Conclusion: Accidents aren't railroad companies' fault.

How to fill gap: should know better → not companies fault

You probably already assumed that naturally. Getting this question right is about explicitly specifying what most people would already assume.

_____

A. This strengthens the idea that the companies aren't to blame, but it doesn't prove 100% that the companies aren't at fault. Maybe there are other things they could do apart from making the gates larger.
B. This tells us what *adults* should do. The question is about whether *railroad companies* are also responsible.
C. **CORRECT.** We know that adults did ignore the warnings. So this answer lets us conclude that adults are fully responsible, and that railroad companies have zero responsibility.
D. Small children are irrelevant. Sure, it'd be *sad* if a child were injured. But that doesn't tell us who is *responsible:* railroad companies or adults.
E. This tells us that there is an upper limit on company responsibility. But the question is about whether companies have any responsibility *at all.*

Question 24

QUESTION TYPE: Flawed Reasoning

CONCLUSION: Well constructed surveys will avoid the problem of people trying to please surveyors.

REASONING: Well constructed surveys will not show which answer the surveyor wants to hear.

ANALYSIS: This question is subtle. It plays on the difference between knowledge and belief.

The stimulus has shown that it's impossible to *know* what answer is expected on a well-constructed survey. I.e. You can't have affirmative, correct *knowledge* of surveyors' expectations.

But that doesn't mean people won't be able to form false *beliefs* about a survey's expectations. And those beliefs could bias answers.

———————————

A. The argument isn't talking about all types of flaws. It's only talking about flaws that result from people trying to meet surveyors' expectations.
B. This would *strengthen* the argument. It shows it's possible for some people to avoid bias in their answers, no matter how surveys are constructed.
C. It doesn't matter if opinion surveyors have expectations. It only matters if respondents *think* surveyors have expectations.
D. This answer talks about people who *know* what answer is expected. Not what answer they *believe* is expected.
   If a well constructed survey reveals no information then you *can't* know what's expected. So this answer is irrelevant to the argument.
E. **CORRECT.** The stimulus made a convincing argument that the surveys wouldn't let you guess what information was expected.
   But that doesn't mean people would realize they can't know. People might falsely believe they knew what was expected. Even if they are wrong about this, it could influence their answers.

Question 25

QUESTION TYPE: Parallel Reasoning

CONCLUSION: TV availability reduces reading by children.

REASONING: When there is TV, children read less. When there is no TV, children read more.

ANALYSIS: This is a simple cause-and-effect argument. The argument shows the effect is present when the cause is there, and the effect goes away when the cause goes away.

———————————

A. **CORRECT.** This matches exactly. It's a simple cause-and-effect argument.
   Cause: money supply fluctuation
   Effect: interest rate fluctuation
   When the cause is present, the effect happens. When the cause isn't present, the effect doesn't happen.
B. This doesn't have the same cause and effect relationship. To parallel the argument, this should have said:
   "When children eat candy, their meals are disrupted. When children don't eat candy, they eat their meals."
C. This has a totally different structure. You can even draw a diagram:
   Industrial pollution → Carbon dioxide → Global warming
   There's no distinction between the presence/absence of a cause.
D. This just lists two factors that affect votes. "A supercilious facial expression" isn't the absence of confidence. Supercilious = arrogant, haughty. To match, this should have said:
   "Confidence affects votes. When candidates are confident, they gain votes. When candidates aren't confident, they lose votes."
E. This just says the relationship goes both ways. It's like saying "The more TV, the less books. The less books, the more TV."
   It sounds similar to the stimulus, but it's not the same thing. It should have said: "The more other activities, the less reading. The fewer other activities, the more reading."

Section II – Reading Comprehension
Passage 1 – Anthropology Video
Questions 1–7

Paragraph Summaries

1. Indigenous people have begun using video to document their own cultures. Anthropological reaction is divided.
2. Some, like James Weiner, think that video will inevitably warp indigenous culture to make it more western.
3. Others, such as Faye Ginsburg argue that indigenous cultures can use Western technology without becoming western. Video may even let indigenous cultures protect themselves from Western influence.
4. Terence Turner's fieldwork in Brazil supports Ginsburg's argument. The Kayapo people have been able to use videos to document their ceremonies and make legal records. The Kayapo videos mirror their ceremonies and culture – they are not Western in style.

Analysis

This passage is a discussion of different theories about the impact of native cultures filming themselves.

The background to this is historic concern about "colonial gaze". That refers to the traditional western-centric view that Western experts would study indigenous societies. Indigenous societies would be watched, and neutral Western experts would be the watchers.

Eventually, people came to be uncomfortable with this idea, and debated it. But this debate was still within Western society.

But now, inexpensive video technology allows indigenous societies to watch themselves. This has led Westerners to debate whether this is a good thing.

There has been a traditional concern in Western circles about Westernizing indigenous societies. It's considered a bad thing if indigenous societies abandon their traditions and adopt those of the West.

This explains Weiner's view. Video technology is Western. And using a technology imposes some constraints in how we use it. Weiner believes that videos will force indigenous people to adopt the values of "realism, immediacy and self-expression."

(Note: Weiner is not saying those values are necessarily bad things. He's saying that those are the *predominant* values of Western society. If indigenous people adopt those three values, then they will displace other values which might have been more useful for them. A society can only have so many values.)

Weiner's opponents, such as Ginsburg, mention the idea of the Noble Savage. This was a concept from European Romantic literature, portraying humans before civilization as idealized, virtuous, happy people.

The concept of the Noble Savage has been ridiculed. Indeed, it does not seem to be based on reality. Indigenous people are human. Every form of society has some good qualities and some bad qualities. It's highly unlikely that society was ideal and perfect before civilization arrived. So Ginsburg thinks that Weiner is Romanticizing indigenous peoples.

While Ginsburg admits that technology is not neutral, they argue that it's likely that indigenous people can use video technology without adopting Western conventions. Indeed, video technology can document and strengthen native traditions.

Ginsburg uses the term "technological determinism". This refers to the idea that if a technology exists, it will inevitably shape society in a certain way. For instance, the idea that if cars exist, we will *inevitably* build suburbs and we have no choice in the matter.

The final paragraph supports Ginsburg's argument that indigenous people can use video without harm. This paragraph also shows that the author agrees with Ginsburg.

In the final paragraph we hear of how the Kayapo use video. They have two uses:

1. They document their ceremonies.
2. They record legal transactions with the Brazilian government.

In the first use, the Kayapo are able to make their videos in a style that mimics their ceremonies. So video technology does *not* inevitably Westernize indigenous cultures.

The point of the second use may be less obvious. You need some outside knowledge. All around the world, colonizing governments have a history of and a reputation for dishonoring agreements made with indigenous peoples.

Often, now, the law of the countries involved may protect the indigenous people against cheating by the government. However, indigenous people often lack proof of the agreement, and are not experienced at dealing with the legal system.

This new video technology allows indigenous people to prove that agreements happened. This will discourage the Brazilian government from cheating, and increase indigenous people's odds of winning a legal case if the government does cheat.

Note: You don't *need* to be familiar with terms like "noble savage", "technological determinism" and "colonial gaze" to do well on reading comprehension. But it helps. If you have several months to study, it is a good idea to read the Economist magazine every week. Doing so will give you a broad background knowledge that will help inform your reading of RC passages.

Question 1

DISCUSSION: As far as I know, this question introduces a new question type. Instead of asking for the main point, it asks you to "summarize the passage".

However in practice I approached this exactly like a main point question. The criteria are identical. You're looking for something that is:

1. True, and
2. A summary of the whole passage

A only summarizes one paragraph. B and D jumble together ideas from the passage to form nonsense answers. E says something almost right, but uses the wrong word. It also is not as good a summary as C is.

————————

A. This is only *Weiner's* argument. So this only covers paragraph 2.
B. Nonsense. Colonial gaze was only mentioned to give context. And colonial gaze is something that *Westerners* do when they observe and document indigenous cultures. That hasn't been eliminated. The difference is that now indigenous cultures can observe and document themselves as well.
C. **CORRECT.** This covers all paragraphs well. Paragraphs 2 and 3 show the division. The final paragraph supports the view in paragraph 3.
D. This doesn't match. It contains some elements present in the passage, but a passage that matched this answer would have a totally different structure.
Example of passage that matches:
Smith shows that video has helped cultures document their traditions.
Jacobs shows that video helps indigenous people pass on their culture to the next generation. However, this video usage is a new phenomenon. We don't know what the effects will be over the next 50-100 years.
E. This is too strong. The Kayapo example doesn't "validate" Ginsburg. Validate means to prove completely correct. The Kayapo merely supports Ginsburg. We don't have enough evidence to make a definitive judgment. See line 47, it merely says "lends credence".

Question 2

DISCUSSION: Faye Ginsburg *completely* rejects Weiner's argument. Lines 34-37 show her opinion. She says Weiner's beliefs are "boilerplate technological determinism".

That's a huge insult. To have a boilerplate view is to have a cliched view that demonstrates no critical reasoning.

A. **CORRECT.** Normally this sort of strong answer isn't correct on the LSAT. But that's because RC passages normally aren't so strongly worded. This one is. Ginsburg thinks that Weiner's argument is completely wrong. So she does fundamentally reject his argument.
B. Reluctant censure would be something like this: "I really like you, and usually you have good ideas, but this time I think you're wrong." It's true that in lines 32-34 Ginsburg concedes a point, but that hardly means she is reluctant in her criticism of Weiner.
C. **Example of answer:** "I don't think that Weiner is right about the Westernizing properties of video. But it's possible. If he is wrong he's not far wrong and it's not a serious error."
D. **Example of answer:** I have no opinion on Weiner's views. Here are the facts, and I will make no claims about them.
E. **Example of answer:** Weiner makes some good points and I'd like to know more.

Question 3

DISCUSSION: The Kayapo used a Western technology to document their performances. But they did not *become* Western in the process.

So to match this, we should look for a group that adopted something from outside the group, but did not fundamentally change.

A. This is the opposite. Video did *not* alter the Kayapo's practices.
B. **CORRECT.** This matches. Latin Americans adopted an outside technique (jazz), but did not abandon their traditions.
C. The Kayapo culture did *not* change. This prediction of a change in the internet goes in the wrong direction.
   Also, prediction had nothing to do with the Kayapo case.
D. This answer involves adapting techniques from the past. But the Kayapo were adopting *modern* video techniques.
   (You might have picked this because the Kayapo are preserving their culture. But preserving your *current* culture and adopting long abandoned techniques from the 1920s are not the same thing.)
E. These European artists were *part of* Western culture. So by rejecting the conventions of Western culture they are doing the opposite of what the Kayapo did. The Kayapo upheld their cultural traditions.

Question 4

DISCUSSION: To answer this, you pretty much just need to read lines 20-21. Western ontology is mentioned on line 20. On line 21 we see that Weiner thinks that it consists of "realism, immediacy and self-expression."

So the right answer will be one of those three words.

―――――――――――

A. Sequential organization is part of *Kayapo* culture. See line 58.
B. Paramount truth value is on line 26. It's not mentioned in the same context as Western ontology.
   Also, since anthropologists are attributing paramount truth to *indigenous* works, this may not necessarily be a purely Western value.
C. **CORRECT.** Self-expression is mentioned directly in line 21. It's part of Western ontology.
D. Colonial gaze is only mentioned in passing in line 2. It has no relation to Western ontology, mentioned on line 20.
E. This is mentioned on line 28. Weiner accuses anthropologists of theoretical naiveté. It's not something that is part of Western ontology, which is mentioned on line 20.

Question 5

DISCUSSION: On this type of question, you should actually be able to point to a specific line that helps answer the question. If you can't, you're probably guessing.

―――――――――――

A. **CORRECT.** Lines 50-52 go into more detail about this. Legal video records allow the Kayapo to have *legally binding* records of their transactions with the Brazilian government. It's implied that these records will help hold the Brazilian government to its agreements. That's what binding means.
B. We don't know. The passage doesn't say where the term comes from.
C. This would be a *long* list. There are a lot of indigenous cultures. Who knows how many have not yet adopted video. This certainly isn't in the passage.
D. Line 35 mentions western objects dating back to the 15th century. But the passage doesn't say *which* objects.
E. Lines 6-8 say inexpensive video equipment is available, but the passage doesn't say why. I expect the answer would be complicated and have to do with technical development, efficient resource extraction, industrial methods, and global shipping.

Question 6

DISCUSSION: Terence Turner was the anthropologist mentioned in the final paragraph who studied the Kayapo's use of video.

Turner thought that the Kayapo were able to use video without modifying their culture. As such Turner *completely disagrees* with Weiner.

A. Turner only talks about the Kayapo. He doesn't talk about other societies.

B. Ridiculous. Everyone in the passage agrees that video technology is widely available. See lines 6-12.

C. Nonsense. Weiner's entire concern is that video will Westernize indigenous peoples, destroying their culture. So Weiner appears to value traditional cultures.

D. CORRECT. This matches. Turner's study of the Kayapo showed that they could adapt video to their culture.
So Turner disagrees with Weiner's view that video will inevitably Westernize indigenous cultures.

E. Turner doesn't mention other technologies, so Turner can't possibly have an opinion about this. This is a gibberish answer.

Question 7

DISCUSSION: You may not be familiar with the term "technological determinism". But you know "technological" and "determine".

It's not a huge stretch to realize that technological determinism is that view that technology will determine how society evolves. Lines 36-37 support this: Ginsburg says that technological determinism is the view that the use of video will make a culture unwittingly Western.

A. This is almost right. But technological determinism isn't the view that technology is *exchanged* between cultures in a predetermined way. It's instead the view that technology will be *used* in a predetermined way.

B. Nonsense. This doesn't match lines 35-37 at all. In those lines the author is talking about how technology affects societies, not anthropologists. And the passage isn't even talking about how anthropologists observe cultures.

C. This is a different view. Lines 35-37 are talking about how technology will *affect* a culture by its use. That could take many forms – nowhere does the passage say that we'll become more and more tech dependent.

D. The passage doesn't even mention ethics. This is a nonsense answer.

E. CORRECT. Lines 35-37 support this. Ginsburg describes Weiner's view that video will inevitably Westernize indigenous cultures as "technological determinism".
That is the view that technology inevitably determines the evolution of society.

Passage 2 – Judicial Bias
Questions 8–14

Paragraph Summaries

1. Current rules on recusal emphasize the appearance of bias, rather than actual bias.
2. Some bias may not be observable. Focussing on the appearance of bias will miss this.
3. We shouldn't have motions to remove judges based on the appearance of bias. Instead we should require written reasons for judgements.
4. There may be bias in written reasons. But as long as there is no problem with the legal reasoning, there is no harm. We can only complain about the result if there is harm.

Analysis

This argument makes some good points, but is also quite naive. I had more trouble than usual on the questions because I found the argument lacking.

The argument starts by explaining how we currently do recusal. Then it argues for a change. There are a lot of details in the passage. It doesn't make sense to memorize them, but you *do* need to know where they are. For instance, if a question asks about how to get a judge to recuse themselves, you should know to look in paragraphs 1 and 2.

Recusal refers to removing yourself from judging a case because you'll be biased. Current regulations focus on the appearance of bias, rather than bias itself (though of course the two often overlap). The passage doesn't explicitly state the reason for this focus on appearance, but the reasons probably are:

1. It is easier to prove the appearance of bias than to prove bias itself. Many cases of appearance will involve actual bias too. Therefore, eliminating appearance will eliminate many cases of actual bias we couldn't otherwise catch.
2. People must believe in the fairness of justice. Allowing the appearance of bias will undermine the justice system.

Of course, the actual reasons aren't important – I'm just speculating. Just know that there would be some argument in favor of the status quo.

The author makes a good criticism of the current recusal system: some cases of bias will never produce an appearance of bias. The current rules will fail to stop these cases.

The author proposes requiring written reasons to eliminate this problem. This may be surprising. You might have assumed that *all* judgements already require written reasons.

Not so. Higher court judgements such as those of the Supreme Court typically have written reasons. But lower court judgements often have only oral reasons and these may not fully lay out the judge's reasoning. Most trials are lower court trials, so this is actually a wide-ranging proposal. Requiring written reasons in all cases would be a major change.

The final paragraph shows why the author thinks written reasons would solve the problem: we could then examine the judge's reasoning to see if it was legally valid. *Even if* there were bias, there could be no harm as long as the reasoning was legally sound. There is something to this. Written reasons would certainly make it easier to get rid of legally wrong judgements that occurred due to bias.

Note: The next two paragraphs explain what's wrong with the proposal. You don't need to know this to get the questions right – this is only a point of interest.

The major problem with this proposal is that there are usually many gray areas in legal judgments. In many cases, it's possible to write a legally sound judgement for or against either side. Therefore bias would let a judge tip the scales without doing anything legally unsound.

For instance, consider sentencing. It might be very clear that a robbery occurred, and no amount of bias would let a judge decide the defendant was innocent. However, bias could show up in the length of sentencing – most sentencing decisions have a range of legally allowable outcomes.

Question 8

DISCUSSION: The second paragraph talks about the weaknesses of the current system. You should look there to prove your answer correct.

A. The passage didn't say this.
B. CORRECT. Lines 15-16 say this.
C. This answer contradicts the passage. Lines 29-31 say transparency is important.
D. This is false. Lines 8-10 say that in some areas you can request that a judge recuse themselves.
E. The author's point is that the appearance of propriety is not what's important. Actual bias is what is important. See lines 16-21.

Question 9

DISCUSSION: The second paragraph discusses the flaws in the current system. I usually re-skim the relevant paragraph before answering a question like this.

All of the wrong answers contradict the passage. Hopefully upon review A is pretty clear. If you got this one wrong you should reread the passage, because missing this question indicates a fundamental lack of comprehension of the material.

That's harsh to write, but it's true. It's important to know where you're falling short.

A. CORRECT. This describes paragraph 2. The first paragraph describes the current approach to bias. The second paragraph says what's wrong with it.
B. The *third* paragraph proposes a solution. The second paragraph doesn't propose any new method.
C. The first paragraph doesn't have a single word of criticism for the current system, and it doesn't mention any problems. Only the *second* paragraph mentions problems.
D. The passage never explains the origins of current recusal rules.
E. Nonsense. Paragraph 2 describes a problem. We don't know yet what the thesis will be. Only paragraph 3 presents the solution to be defended.

Question 10

DISCUSSION: If you go back to the passage and read the *entire* sentence quoted, this question is easy. The quotation in the question itself leaves out the start of the sentence: "*Under the law,* a right of recourse...."

So the author thinks this principle is well established in law.

———————————

A. CORRECT. See the analysis above. The full sentence quoted says this pretty directly.
B. Nonsense. Lines 25-26 define the function of the law: "the settlement of normative disputes." The quoted lines aren't part of this.
C. The author doesn't talk about tools judges can use to disguise their real reasoning.
D. In the final paragraph, the author argues that bias without harm is fine because there's only a right to recourse if there's harm.
So the author thinks this is *fair,* not unfair.
E. Nonsense. In the fourth paragraph the author is making a *new* proposal. They think this right of recourse is central to their *new* idea, not the old system.

Question 11

DISCUSSION: Paragraph 2 discusses the weakness of the current rules. On this type of question you should reread or reskim the paragraph first to prephrase the weakness. This will let you move through the answers very quickly.

———————————

A. Actually, line 12 says the guidelines are vague, not rigid.
B. Nonsense. Judges could very well make their reasoning transparent, *and* withdraw if there was the appearance of bias.
The author doesn't think the second bit is necessary if there is transparency, but the two ideas certainly aren't incompatible.
C. CORRECT. Lines 22-24 say pretty much exactly this.
D. There's no conflict. Professional codes are only mentioned on line 3, to specify that codes focus on the appearance of impropriety.
The passage never says whether a statute could place a judge in conflict with a professional code. If the passage *had* said that, it would be in paragraph 1 – but that information simply isn't there.
E. This is silly. You don't get to disqualify a judge merely because you *request* it. No legal system would ever make such a ridiculous guarantee. You have to *prove* your point before a judge will withdraw.

Question 12

DISCUSSION: The final paragraph covers the proposal for written reasons. You should reread that before answering the question (or skim it). That will let you move through the answers *much* faster.

———————————

A. Actually, the author says judges *could* be biased if they provide written reasons. However the bias will not matter if the reasons are legally sound. See lines 45-48.

B. CORRECT. The final paragraph pretty much says this. See lines 46-48. Those lines say that if people can't spot errors, then there's no problem. This implies that it would be possible to find faulty reasoning, because bad reasoning *is* a problem.

C. Not so. Written reasons *could* conceal the real reasoning, but the author doesn't say this will usually happen.

D. Who knows what the public will think? The author never mentions the public.

E. The author suggests this is *less* likely. The written reasons, if legally sound, will help a judge show that there were no ill effects from bias.

Question 13

DISCUSSION: The final paragraph addresses the possibility that judges could use legal reasoning to hide their actual reasons.

Example: A judge wants to find a defendant guilty because the judge doesn't like their clothes. However, the judge uses evidence and legal arguments to argue the defendant is guilty.

The author argues this isn't a problem. It's fine for judges to use silly, biased reasons to convict, *if* they can also provide compelling legal reasoning to support their decisions.

———————————

A. No, the final paragraph is referring to reasons for judgements, not reasons for recusal.

B. The author never mentions people without legal training. On lines 46-48 they mention people *with* legal knowledge, but that doesn't mean the judgements couldn't also be understood by regular people.

C. CORRECT. Suppose a judge convicted because they hated someone's attitude, but wrote a compelling legal argument for conviction. The real reason for conviction would be the judge's hatred.
However the author argues this is acceptable if the legal reasoning is sound.

D. No, this refers to the written reasons. We won't know the *real* reasons for a judgment.

E. Rubbish. The passage doesn't even mention central legal principles.

Question 14

DISCUSSION: The current approach depends on the appearance of bias. Judges can step down if they want, and in some areas people can request judges step down. (See paragraph 1)

However, this will not catch all cases of bias. See lines 22-24.

Further, since the rules focus on the *appearance* of bias, it's possible that some unbiased judges will be asked to step down.

———————————

A. The author never tells us what the public believes. They may think that eliminating the appearance of bias is enough.
B. The author never tells us what judges believe.
C. The first part isn't supported. Current rules focus on the *appearance* of bias. So it's possible that many unbiased judges are removed because of a possible appearance of bias.
D. The first part isn't supported. Lines 22-24 say that the current system may not catch many cases of actual bias.
E. **CORRECT.** See the analysis above. There is reason to believe that some unbiased judges will be removed, and some biased judges will be allowed to remain.
This is because in some cases a judge may actually be unbiased and yet appear biased. And in other cases the judge may appear unbiased but actually be biased.

Passage 3 – Ethics (comparative)
Questions 15–20

Paragraph Summaries

Passage A

1. St. Augustine said we shouldn't lie just because someone is a liar.
2. But some say that fairness allows us to lie to liars.
3. There are two questions: 1. Are we allowed to lie to liars? 2. If so, should we?
4. Consider a harmless liar. They have no right to the truth. But we must also consider whether we hurt *ourselves* if we lie to him.

Passage B

1. Kant said that if someone rational acts in a certain way towards others, then that person implies that it's fine to act that way towards them.
2. Some say this means we *must* treat people how they treat others.
3. But actually we are only *allowed* to treat people the way they treat others. We don't *have* to.

Analysis

These ethical passages always take a lot of writing to say very little. My summaries above are pretty much all that's in the passages.

I don't really think there's very much to analyze here. You don't need to know anything that's not in the summaries. At most you need to know *where* information is, in order to prove or disprove answers.

The one thing that deserves consideration is the idea of a rational being in the second passage. The entire second passage is based upon people acting rationally. If, for some reason, we couldn't say that someone was a rational being, then the argument doesn't apply.

Question 15

DISCUSSION: Both passages are about whether we should treat others the way *they* treat others.

A. Neither passage really considers harm as the main principle. The first passage mentions a harmless liar, but only to make a different point.
B. Neither passage talks about the distinction between legal wrongs and moral wrongs.
C. **CORRECT.** The first passage is about whether to lie to a liar. The second passage is about whether to treat a rational being the way they treat others.
D. The second passage talks about duties and rights. But the author is not interested in *defining* the difference. The author assumes we already know this difference.
E. Only passage two talks about rational beings. And it doesn't say whether all wrongdoers should be treated as rational.

Question 16

DISCUSSION: Remember, this question is looking for something that *is in* A, and not in B.

You should look for the first part first. It's easy to prove that something is in a passage. It's harder to prove that something isn't.

A. CORRECT. Lines 24-26 in passage A talk about how you can harm yourself and others by lying. Passage B doesn't talk about harm directly. On lines 52-54 the author does discuss whether or not a rational being could *object* to being treated as they treated others. But objecting is not the same thing as harm, and if you *can't* object you certainly can't claim harm.

I'll note that this answer seems *a bit* fuzzier than most, as the second passage is certainly talking about what's right and wrong to do. But things can be right and wrong independent of whether they cause harm.

B. In passage A lines 24-26 talk about the consequences of lying (i.e. of reciprocating). They don't talk about the consequences of *not reciprocating*.

C. Only passage B talks about rational beings.

D. Only passage B talks about who is owed respect (lines 40-46).

E. Neither passage mentions any specific instance or actual people. These are abstract, hypothetical passages far removed from actual examples.

Question 17

DISCUSSION: This question diverges slightly from RC trends. Normally, it's possible to explicitly prove answers with line references. However, while I think the right answer is 100% correct, I can't point to a pair of lines that proves it definitively.

Specifically, the right answer describes what both passages are doing, but using different words. Neither passage said "unreasonable consequences". It's fine to use different words to refer to the same concept. The LSAT expects you to be comfortable with using synonyms and calling something by a different but equivalent name.

A. I was tempted by this because both passages disagree with opposing arguments. But that's not the same thing as "anticipating and refuting" objections, which is a very specific form of argument.

I've made an example below that matches the structure in this answer. It has the same content, but the order is different. In the stimulus the author *started* with the theory they objected to, and ended with their conclusion. In my example, I start with the conclusion, reject it, then refute the rejection.

Example of anticipating and refuting rejection: We should lie to someone just because they are a liar. This is my theory.
You might object that they deserve it. But that's not sufficient justification on its own.

B. An analogy is when you compare one situation to another situation. There are no analogies in either passage. For instance, the pathological liar in passage A is an *example,* not an analogy.

C. Passage A focusses on a specific case in lines 19-27. But passage B doesn't use any specific cases.

D. CORRECT. In passage A, the view is the eye for an eye view described in paragraph 2: we should treat people as they treat others.
The final paragraph shows that this view has unreasonable consequences: the view implies that we should lie to a harmless liar, even though by doing so we could harm ourselves or society.

Line 38 says "from this it might be concluded" that we have a *duty* to treat people as they treat others. This is the unreasonable consequence that the author disagrees with. In lines 41-46 the author says it seems "excessive" to completely mirror people.

As I wrote in the analysis, you can't literally prove this answer with words in the passage. You have to use common sense to see that in both cases the results described in each passage could be fairly and correctly described as "unreasonable consequences".

E. This didn't happen at all.
Example of argument: Most people say that lying is to say things that aren't true. But I believe lying is when we say things we don't feel. This is true because....etc.

Question 18

DISCUSSION: The right answer for this type of question should be *clearly supported*. The wrong answers will all be clearly wrong. If you have to stretch to justify an answer, it probably isn't the right one.

Look to the passage if you're uncertain. Passage A very clearly supports C, in lines 23-27. Once you spot those lines, it's easy to choose it.

A. Rational beings were only discussed in passage B.
B. Neither passage argued that we have a *duty* to treat people as they treat others. Both authors instead argued that we have *the right* to do so.
C. CORRECT. Lines 23-27 say this directly. A pathological liar has no right to the truth, but we might still want to avoid lying, as we could harm ourselves by lying, or harm others.
D. Line 26 says other circumstances have to be "taken into account". So the author of passage A is not saying "don't lie". They're saying "consider carefully whether to lie to a liar". This implies that it some cases lying to a liar may indeed be justified.
So this answer is unsupported.
E. Passage A never talks about innocent people or whether they always deserve innocence.

Question 19

DISCUSSION: You should reread the quoted lines to prephrase what they're talking about.

- Lines 11-13 are talking about your right not to have people do bad things *to you*.
- Lines 50 is talking about your right *to do* things to other people.

I really don't know how to "explain" the wrong answers. They simply don't appear in the passages. They're nonsense answers throwing in words your brain associates with ethics and rights. They have zero worth.

It's no coincidence that this question is long and the right answer is E. If an answer seems to suck, move past it. Unless an answer seems obviously correct, don't give *any* answer serious consideration until you read them all. Often D or E will be obviously right, so you need to avoid wasting 30-40 seconds on A or B.

A. The passages don't distinguish between legal and moral rights.
B. The passages don't talk about benefits given by an authority figure.
C. The passages don't distinguish between group rights and individual rights.
D. In passage *A* the author is talking about rights that can be lost if you behave badly.
Neither passage talks about rights that cannot be given up.
E. CORRECT. Passage A is talking about bullies and liars *forfeiting* the right to be treated well. So this use of "right" refers to right *to be treated* in a certain way by others.
Passage B bit is less clear. You need to know the sense of the whole second paragraph. The paragraph starts by saying that we may have a duty to treat people the way they treat others. However, line 50 says we do not *have* to do so. Instead we have the right to do so, if we wish. So viewed as a whole this part of passage B is talking about what we can do to others.
"Licensed to engage in" means "allowed to do."

Question 20

DISCUSSION: The Kantian argument in the first paragraph of passage B is that if a rational actor treats others a certain way, we have the right to treat that actor the same way. Taking the first paragraph on its own, we may even have a *duty* to treat people as they do others. (See lines 38-41. The rest of passage B contradicts this argument, but this question is only talking about the first paragraph.)

Passage A is saying that in many cases we *should not* lie to a harmless pathological liar. So this seems incompatible with the argument in the first paragraph of passage B.

Except....passage B only applies to *rational* actors. So we could get around the incompatibility by saying that the pathological liar is not rational. Passage B doesn't say how to treat irrational people.

This is almost like a logical reasoning question. This style of question has been appearing more frequently on reading comprehension.

A. The Kantian argument never said whether *our* behavior should be rational. It only talks about how to *treat* a rational actor.
   Also this is very much like E. Both answers can't be right.

B. **CORRECT.** If this is true, then the Kantian argument doesn't apply to a pathological liar. The Kantian argument only applied to rational actors. See lines 28-32.

C. This answer tells us that the Kantian argument *does* apply, since the liar is rational. We therefore have the right to lie, according to the Kantian argument.

D. This was already included in the Kantian argument. It doesn't match the excerpt from passage A, which says we may not have reason to lie to a liar.

E. The bit about low standards is just taking an irrelevant phrase from paragraph 1 of passage A (lines 3-4). Adding an irrelevant concept from the passage makes this answer feel familiar to your brain. Familiar things feel correct.
   This answer can't help us reconcile the two arguments. "Low standards" has no logical link to passage B – that passage is talking about how to treat others, and doesn't mention "standards".

Passage 4 – Glass flow
Questions 21–27

Paragraph Summaries

1. Despite myths to the contrary, glass won't flow downwards unless heated to the glass transition temperature.
2. A new study confirms that glass flow is not the cause of thicker windows in medieval cathedrals. Glass will very slowly flow downwards – but on a timescale beyond the age of the universe.
3. Even the glass that flows most easily, germanium oxide, would take trillions of years to produce the effects seen in medieval windows.
4. Window thickness differences probably come from old glass manufacturing methods. Old methods used to produce thicker ends. These ends were placed at the bottom for stability.

Analysis

This passage has a lot of details which I couldn't include in the paragraph summaries. You don't need to know all these details or even necessarily understand them. But you should know where to find them.

I know a bit more than what I wrote about each paragraph. For instance if someone mentions "impurities in glass" I remember that's in paragraph 3, when the author was talking about composition of medieval church windows.

The more of the science you understand, the better you'll do. But you don't *need* to understand everything to get all the questions.

My strategy on these passages is to read things I don't understand over again. Maybe you won't get a perfect understanding, but you'll at least understand more than before, and this will help you make sense of the rest of the passage + the questions.

The gist of this passage is that regular people falsely believe that glass flows like a liquid. Important: Glass researchers do not share this belief. See lines 1-4 for both facts.

So Zanotto's research is not proving anything that glass experts didn't already know.

Zanotto's research is interesting, and it provides new data to support existing beliefs, but it hasn't changed our view of glass.

I'll explain the physical structure of glass, then cover Zanotto's research.

Some key facts about glass:

- Liquid and solid glass have similar structures. Their atoms aren't in a crystal structure. (Lines 9-12)
- Liquid and solid glass are *thermodynamically* different. This means they flow differently.
- Glass doesn't freeze from liquid to solid. Instead, it has a transition temperature.
- When sufficiently cooled, liquid glass keeps its atomic structure, but becomes physically like a solid.

Basically liquid and solid glass have similar structures. But solid glass behaves like a solid. Heat glass hot enough, and it starts behaving like a liquid.

However, a lot of people believe in a myth: they think that solid glass flows downwards because it has a liquid structure. (Remember, glass experts do *not* share this belief. See lines 1-4 "To glass researchers it seems strange....")

This belief is false, and that's what Zanotto's research helps confirm.

Paragraphs 2 and 3 describe Zanotto's research. He helped conclusively confirm that it would take a *long* time for glass to flow downwards. You don't really need to know the details of these paragraphs beyond that.

The final paragraph explains the real reason that glass is thicker at the bottom of many older windows: past manufacturing techniques produced uneven window panes, and the thick ends were placed downwards.

Question 21

DISCUSSION: When you read a passage, you should always ask: "Why is the author telling me this?" That will help you filter out wrong answers. E is pretty obviously the main point if you had a good understanding of the passage and thought about why the author wrote what they wrote.

The wrong answers are typically either wrong or minor details. A and B are just random facts from the passage. They aren't the main point. C and D are actually false.

_____

A. This is just a random fact from the passage. The overall point is that Zanotto's research supports the original understanding that glass doesn't flow down much at all at low temperatures.

B. This is just a fact from the fourth paragraph. It explains why old windows have thicker bottoms. It was manufacturing techniques, not flow rates.

C. Nonsense. Lines 39-43 show that Zanotto is confirming earlier studies. There were no "years of investigations" into glass flow, or "a common misunderstanding" about glass.
Lines 1-4 show that ordinary people have a myth about glass, but glass researchers haven't been confused.

D. This answer is false! Lines 31-34 show that it would take trillions of years for glass to sag. Glass motion is *not* "one of several factors" that's contributed to thick glass bottoms.

E. **CORRECT.** This covers everything. Paragraph 1 discusses the common belief. Paragraphs 2 and 3 show the study that debunks the belief. The final paragraph shows the real reason.
This answer focusses mainly on the final paragraph, but it does cover everything.

Question 22

DISCUSSION: On this type of question, the right answer will be something that you can literally point to in the passage. If you can't do that, you're guessing.

The wrong answers take terms from the passage, but terms that were just mentioned as asides. There is no information in the passage that will answer the questions in the wrong answers.

Familiar terms feel more "right" to the brain. This is a known psychological bias. Know that you should move through answers rapidly if you're only considering them because a term feels familiar. Either find the term in the passage to prove the answer, or move on.

_____

A. Lines 46-49 show that the passage lumps all pre-19th century glass blowing into the same category. The author didn't differentiate between 17th century and medieval techniques.

B. **CORRECT.** The fourth paragraph covers this. One way that modern techniques differ is that modern window glass is made by floating liquid glass on molten tin (lines 55-56).

C. The passage never mentions pre-medieval windows.

D. The passage only mentions germanium oxide once, on lines 32-35. It's given as an example of the fastest flowing glass. The author never says whether it's used in churches.
The point of mentioning it was to show that *even* the fastest flowing glass is incredibly slow.

E. Lines 35-36 say that there were impurities in medieval glass, but the passage doesn't say how they got there.

Question 23

DISCUSSION: Lines 20-23 show that the author completely agrees with Zanotto's study. The author says the study debunks the popular myth of glass flow. That means the author thinks the study is correct.

While the myth was persistent, glass experts did not believe in the myth (lines 1-4). So Zanotto's work, while correct and interesting, is not saying anything that glass experts didn't already believe.

However, lines 39-43 show that Zanotto's work does provide some new data. Previously, it seems scientists had only reasoned through the possibilities. Now Zanotto's work provides actual data proving them correct.

———————

A. **CORRECT.** See the analysis above. The three excerpts I quote, in combination, show that this is the correct answer. Zanotto provided data to support a belief that scientists already held.
B. The second half of this is right. Lines 1-4 show that glass researchers thought this was settled. But Zanotto merely confirmed their account. So there's no new research needed.
C. Lines 7-10 say that the origins of the myth are unclear. Zanotto's study was based on confirming that the myth is false. He didn't look into the history of the myth.
D. Which two views? Don't choose an answer like this unless you can very clearly find the two views and spell out how they're incompatible.
E. Nonsense. This passage appears to have completely explained the phenomenon of why glass is thicker at the bottom. Zanotto showed that it's not flow speed (paragraphs 2 and 3). And then the author shows the real explanation was glass making techniques (paragraph 4).

Question 24

DISCUSSION: Lines 9-19 cover the atomic structure of glass. Liquid and solid glass are not the same. When solid glass is heated to the glass transition temperature, it changes to a liquid glass structure. Below that, it has the properties of a solid.

Lines 39-43 imply that when glass is heated to the transition temperature, it will flow. ("To have more than a negligible rate of flow" implies that glass will develop faster flow at increasing temperatures.)

Honestly, it takes a lot of work to eliminate answers here. It's not worth the effort to conclusively prove them wrong. I think the right answer is pretty straightforward if you got the main idea of the passage: glass doesn't flow as a solid, will flow if heated. Pick D, move on, figure the rest out on review.

———————

A. Actually lines 18-19 say that glass behaves as a solid unless it is heated to the glass transition temperature.
B. This answer contradicts the passage. Lines 31-34 say that it would take solid glass trillions of years to sag.
C. Lines 10-19, taken as a whole, say that glass will be a solid below its transition temperature, and a liquid above the transition temperature.
   The author says that "it takes on the properties of a solid" when glass passes below the transition temperature, which implies that glass had liquid properties above the the transition temperature.
D. **CORRECT.** This is strongly supported. Glass is a liquid above the transition temperature, and liquids flow. Lines 39-43 say that glass will have a more than negligible flow rate when heated above 350 degrees celsius.
E. Nonsense. Lines 9-10 say that the atoms in glass are *not* arranged in a fixed crystalline structure. This doesn't change above or below the transition temperature. (See lines 10-12: liquid and solid glass have very similar structures, but behave differently.)

Question 25

DISCUSSION: This question is asking for the reason people falsely think that glass flows. Lines 1-4 show that *glass experts* didn't have this false believe. So it is *regular people* who have this false belief.

So the right answer probably won't be too technical. There has to be something in there that regular people could form a misunderstanding about.

Also, only paragraph 1 talks about people's beliefs. That means the support must come from that paragraph. Any answer mentioning medieval glass or glass manufacturing, for example, is wrong because the author never told us what people think about those things.

Incidentally, I spent an incredible amount of time trying to explain this question. I couldn't for the life of me see how the right answer was supported by the passage.

Turns out I misread the question. I thought it said "which of the following explains why the myth occurred?". But actually it's asking which *false assumption* people believed about glass. (I got this right timed, then read it wrong when writing the explanation.)

Why am I boring you with this information? Because if it can happen to me, it can happen to you. If you're totally stuck on question, moving through the answers slowly one by one, you've done something wrong. Take a few deep breaths, and reread the question. If it still doesn't make sense, move on and come back later at the end of the passage if you have time.

———————————

A. It's highly unlikely that regular people would create a myth because they thought glass was crystalline rather than amorphous.
In any case, crystals don't flow. So if people believed this answer then they would also think that glass *does not* flow.
(Line 17 shows that molten glass has an amorphous structure. That's what lets it flow!)

B. CORRECT. I found this easy to choose from intuition, but hard to explicitly justify with the passage text. Bear with me.
Lines 8-10 show that the persistent belief probably came from a misunderstanding about glasses's structure. People *correctly* understand that glass isn't a crystal structure. However, they misunderstand what this means. Line 4 show that glass' lack of crystal structure makes people think it flows downward like a viscous liquid. However, this is wrong. Lines 17-19 show that cooled glass behaves as a solid, even though it has an amorphous structure.

Phew. I don't think you needed to have all those citations to get this question right. My prephrase of this question in timed conditions was "something something people think glass structure flows, but that's wrong"
And that worked. It's very helpful to go through all these citations on review, as it will help your timed work. But don't think you need to know all this in real time. It took me 5-10 minutes to write the explanation for this question.

C. Only paragraph 1 talks about people's beliefs. We're never told what people think about medieval glass or glass manufacturing methods.

D. The passage doesn't mention people's beliefs about transition temperatures, or about medieval glass. For people to have a misapprehension about something, we need to know what they think of it.

E. This was a trap answer. It gets things backwards. It says people think that liquid and solid glass are thermodynamically dissimilar.
But actually, people mistakenly believe that liquid and solid glass are thermodynamically *similar*. That's why they think solid glass flows downwards: they believe it behaves like a liquid.
The full error in lines 10-14 is this: People see that liquid and solid glass are structurally similar, so they mistakenly think that liquid and solid glass are thermodynamically *similar*.

Question 26

DISCUSSION: People thought glass windows were thicker at the bottom because of physical properties of glass (See paragraph 1). The actual cause was likely the manufacturing process (see paragraph 4).

Every wrong answer mentions people's beliefs *about* the manufacturing process. But in the passage, we don't know people's opinion of the manufacturing process.

That's why B is right. It's the only answer that blames people *ignorance* of manufacturing techniques.

A. This doesn't match. The author never told us what people think about glass manufacturing.

B. **CORRECT.** This matches. People thought the thickness of the bottom of glass windows was due to the structure of glass.
   People were unaware that the actual cause was the manufacturing techniques.

C. Same as A. Manufacturing was the actual cause (paragraph 4), but the author never said people had any beliefs about manufacturing. The author only mentioned people's beliefs about the structure of glass itself (paragraph 1).

D. Same as A and C. This answer mentioned people's beliefs about how something was made. But in the passage we only know people's beliefs about the physical structure and properties of glass (paragraph 1).

E. Differences in modern and historical glass production are only mentioned in paragraph 4. We're not told what people believe about these manufacturing methods.

Question 27

DISCUSSION: The transition temperature is mentioned in two places:

- Lines 13-17: The transition temperature is a few hundred degrees celsius.
- Lines 41-43: Glass would need to be heated to *at least* 350 degrees to flow more rapidly.

So the passage doesn't define transition temperature in precise detail. But the "*at least* 350 degrees" implies that the hotter glass is, the faster it flows. And the 350 degrees is the bare minimum for glass to start flowing at a noticeable rate.

A. You might have picked this because you remembered that impurities in medieval glass make it flow more quickly (lines 35-36). There are two problems with this:
   * These impurities may only affect viscosity/flow speed, not transition temperature itself.
   * The impurities *increase* flow speed. So if anything, they *lower* transition temperature. This answer says they raise transition temperature.

B. This answer defies common sense. People have been working with and melting glass for thousands of years. It would be insane to believe that glassworkers didn't know the transition temperature of glass.
   If an answer seems insane in the real world, it's probably not the right answer. You need *extremely* clear justification from the passage to pick an answer like this.

C. **CORRECT.** See the discussion section above. 350 degrees is the bare minimum for glass to start flowing. So the upper extreme of the transition temperature must be much higher.

D. This contradicts the passage. Once glass passes the transition temperature, it begins to flow (lines 41-43). Glass can even become liquid and float (see line 56).

E. This isn't supported. Lines 41-43 appear to be saying that *all* glass must be heated above 350 degrees celsius to flow even a little.

42

Section 3 – Logical Reasoning

Question 1

QUESTION TYPE: Complete the Argument

CONCLUSION: Resisting new technology in industry is futile in the long run.

REASONING: If a firm resists new technology, then it will eventually be replaced by a different firm that did adopt new technology.

ANALYSIS: This passage is about how some firms and workers resist new technology in order to preserve jobs. But firms that do this for too long will go out of business, destroying all their jobs.

Therefore, the logical conclusion of the argument is that resisting new technology will not help preserve jobs in the long run.

———————————

A. This is a confusing answer. What it actually says is: "Resisting technology will help create job security for workers".
That's the opposite of what the argument is saying!
B. This contradicts the first sentence. The first sentence says that both skilled and unskilled people are affected by tech change. Those who can adapt to new technology prosper, while others lose their jobs.
C. **CORRECT.** This makes sense. Firms can resist job loss for a time by resisting new technology, but eventually those firms will go out of business, losing all jobs.
D. The argument supports the opposite conclusion: resisting technology will lead to a loss of jobs in the long run.
E. Nonsense. The argument is saying that resisting technology leads to job loss. So it doesn't make sense to prioritize it!

Question 2

QUESTION TYPE: Necessary Assumption

CONCLUSION: The Hydro is probably doing well because people want to seem environmentally friendly.

REASONING: The Hydro has no advantages over competing fuel efficient cars.

ANALYSIS: The argument has given us *zero* evidence to support buying the Hydro. As far as we know, it's the same as other cars. The conclusion says people buy it to seem environmentally friendly. So it's a necessary assumption that the Hydro has an environmentally friendly reputation. (Even though it's no better for the environment)

———————————

A. All that matters is that Hydro sales are *rising*. The Hydro doesn't have to be number 1.
Negation: The Hydro is doing incredibly well, and sales are increasing faster than all other cars. However, the Hydro is not yet the top selling fuel-efficient car.
B. **CORRECT.** If this isn't true, then there's no reason that people would buy the Hydro to seem environmentally friendly.
Negation: The Hydro does not have a reputation for being more environmentally friendly than its competitors.
C. This *weakens* the argument by providing an alternate explanation for the rising sales. A necessary assumption answer should *strengthen* the argument if true.
D. This doesn't tell us *why* people buy Hydros. In fact it may weaken the argument because it implies people may be buying Hydros in order to mimic their neighbors. (Rather than for environmental reasons)
E. You might have picked this because you thought Hydro buyers were covering for their lack of interest in the environment by buying the Hydro – but that's a HUUUUGE stretch and definitely not necessary.
Negation: Buyers of the Hydro have the same interest in the environment as do purchasers of other fuel efficient cars.

Question 3

QUESTION TYPE: Principle – Justify

CONCLUSION: It would be unfair to dismiss Louise's McBride's complaint.

REASONING: McBride's complaint was filed on the wrong form. But a government employee incorrectly provided McBride with that form.

ANALYSIS: Principle-justify questions depend on your ability to separate fact from moral principles.

You might have thought "This is a good argument. That poor woman shouldn't fail just because a government employee made a mistake".

To strengthen the argument, you just need to state that principle explicitly: "Complaints shouldn't be denied on a technicality if the error was due to a government employee's actions."

Or something like that. Making the moral principle explicit is what lets you connect the facts in the evidence to the moral judgement in the conclusion.

—————————

A. This doesn't help us. We want to prove that the complaint shouldn't be dismissed even though the wrong form was used.
B. The issue wasn't that the form was hard to complete. The issue was that the bureaucrat gave Louise the *wrong* form.
C. **CORRECT.** This matches. Louise's mistake was due to the government agency's error. This answer lets us conclude that we shouldn't reject her complaint on account of that.
D. We don't know why the employee gave the incorrect form. It might not have been due to complex procedures. Maybe the employee was just tired.
E. The argument *supports* the complaint. But this answer tells us how to *dismiss* complaints against business.
(Adding an extra condition for filing complaints always makes complaints harder, not easier)

Question 4

QUESTION TYPE: Most Strongly Supported

FACTS:
1. Healthy birds generally have larger spleens than sickly birds do.
2. Birds killed by predators tend to have smaller spleens.

ANALYSIS: It sounds like predators kill sickly birds more often. This is probably because sickly birds are easier to kill.

There are some ways you could cast doubt on this conclusion. But this is a most strongly supported question. You just need to conclude what seems probable. It doesn't need to be 100% certain.

—————————

A. This doesn't follow. It might be *harder* to kill healthy birds, but that doesn't mean it's impossible.
B. This doesn't follow. It's *more common* for sickly birds to die from predators. But that doesn't mean that *most* sickly birds die from predators. That'd be a slaughter!
C. Hard to say. The predators might be catching sickly birds simply because sickly birds are slower. The predators might not realize their easy catches are due to sickness.
D. **CORRECT.** This is well supported. Birds with small spleens tend to be more sickly, and we know small-spleened birds are killed more often.

You might have noticed there are a couple of ways this answer could be not true. Doesn't matter. On a most strongly supported question, you're just looking for something probable. It doesn't have to be 100% ironclad.
E. This goes too far. It's possible that there are other causes of sickness. In fact it's even possible that sickness causes small spleen size, rather than the reverse.

Question 5

QUESTION TYPE: Paradox

PARADOX: Home ownership is linked with prosperity. But there is high unemployment in areas with high home ownership.

ANALYSIS: You're allowed to use common sense on the LSAT, to form hypotheses. Most of the LSAT is based on real life situations.

I've read about this situation in the Economist. Articles I read there mentioned that home ownership can make it harder to switch jobs, because you can't move as easily. Therefore, home ownership can encourage unemployment.

I went into the answers *expecting* to find that prephrase. If it wasn't there, I would have considered the other answers with an open mind. But having that prephrase significantly sped me up.

If you have several months to study, I recommend the Economist to gain breath of knowledge. You'll see a lot of stuff from the magazine appear in the LSAT.

———————————

A. **CORRECT.** If you can't move to a new job, then you may remain unemployed longer.
(If you're wondering how people got the house in the first place, they probably had jobs in the past. It's just that the house makes it harder to find a new job if you lose yours.)

B. This suggests that there are *more* jobs in areas with homes. That deepens the paradox.

C. This suggests the paradox exists in many different countries. But it doesn't *explain* the paradox.

D. This is a reason that homeowners are *more likely* to find jobs. It deepens the paradox.

E. This explains why home ownership is associated with wealth (economic security). When people are wealthy, they decide to buy a house.
But this *doesn't* explain why homeownership is associated with lack of a job. Losing your job is associated with economic *insecurity*.

Question 6

QUESTION TYPE: Strengthen

HYPOTHESIS: Scientists think that when tobacco hatchworms eat nightshades first, their taste receptors get used to indioside D, which is only found in nightshades. Then nothing else tastes good.

BACKGROUND: Newborn tobacco hatchworms that eat nightshades first don't eat any other plants. But if hatchworms eat other plants first, they'll continue eating nightshades *and* other plants.

ANALYSIS: The scientists have made a plausible hypothesis, but they haven't really provided evidence to support their idea. To support this, we ought to test the hypothesis that indioside D and taste are the cause.

For example, we could try putting indioside D in another plant and seeing if hookworms eat it. Or try feeding hookworms nightshades with the indioside D removed. That would help test the hypothesis that indioside D is the real factor.

The right answer supports the taste hypothesis by showing that hookworms change their eating habits when taste is gone.

———————————

A. This explains nothing. From the stimulus we had no reason to say whether or not some nightshades would be better than others.

B. **CORRECT.** This is incredibly strong evidence. Taste was hypothesized as a cause, and this shows that hatchworms change their eating patterns when taste is removed.
This doesn't prove that indioside D is the cause of the taste bonding, but this is only a strengthen question – no need to prove the argument 100%.

C. This explains *why* tobacco hatchworms might eat nightshades first, but it doesn't explain why they *only* eat nightshades after that.

D. This *weakens* the hypothesis. The cause of the hookworm eating patterns might be one of the other chemicals, rather than indioside D.

E. It's highly unlikely that taste receptors would only respond to 1-2 chemicals. We could already assume this was true. And this *doesn't* explain anything about indioside D.

Question 7

QUESTION TYPE: Flawed Reasoning

CONCLUSION: My boss was wrong to say I should have included *more* detail.

REASONING: *Too much* detail is boring.

ANALYSIS: There is a big difference between *more* and *too much*. It's possible the employee could have added more detail without adding too much detail.

A. The employee wasn't arguing that their boss is usually wrong. They were only saying the boss was wrong in this specific case.
B. **CORRECT.** This is a major distinction. The employee might have been able to add more detail without adding too much.
C. The employee wasn't saying their presentation is guaranteed not to lead to wandering attention. They were only saying that too much detail wouldn't be the cause of wandering attention.
D. This is a different flaw.
   Example of flaw: My boss was wrong once. So they are always wrong.
E. This type of answer is almost never right. You have to be able to say *exactly* what the two different meanings are to choose this type of answer.
   Example of flaw: The public isn't interested in court proceedings. Therefore, court proceeding aren't a matter of public interest.
   (The first sense means boring vs. interesting. The second sense means something of importance to public affairs.)

Question 8

QUESTION TYPE: Identify the Conclusion

CONCLUSION: The Clemens scandal is an example of how the the media is too nice to public figures.

REASONING: The media thought Clemens was honest. As such they didn't bother investigating him. It turns out that Clemens was dishonest.

ANALYSIS: The gist of the argument is that the media is too deferential to public figures like Clemens. Clemens isn't the point – he is just an example demonstrating this point about the media. Note that the third sentence says "This [Clemens' corruption] *demonstrates*". Media failure is the real point of the argument.

Ideally, you should be able to figure that out just from reading it. That's the end goal of your LSAT studies: to figure out conclusions intuitively. But if you're still having trouble, I've identified some words below that indicate conclusions and evidence.

"This demonstrates" indicates that the sentence is a conclusion and the previous sentence supports it.

"Even....admitted" indicates that the sentence is evidence, supporting the conclusion in the previous sentence. Here, "even" shows that someone we would expect to object (the newspaper editor) agrees with the author.

A. This fact supports the conclusion. Clemens was *not* honest, so the fact that the media portrayed him as honest shows the media is too deferential.
B. This is *true*, and a very tempting answer. But the point is that Clemens' case demonstrates *how* the media are too deferential. The scandal is just evidence showing the excess deference.
C. **CORRECT.** The point of the argument is that Clemens' case demonstrates this fact.
D. This is just evidence supporting the conclusion that the media is too deferential.
E. The argument said the local *media* is too deferential. But this answer only talks about how the local *newspaper* treats public figures. The media is bigger than the newspaper.
   Also the conclusion is not just that Clemens' case is typical. It's that Clemens' case shows excess *deference*.

46

Question 9

QUESTION TYPE: Parallel Reasoning

CONCLUSION: Life has never existed on the moon.

REASONING: If life had existed on the moon, there would be evidence. We haven't found evidence so far.

ANALYSIS: Absence of evidence is not evidence of absence. Something can exist even if we haven't found it yet. That's all there is to this argument. Often the error is quite simple.

———————————

A. The stimulus had *absence of evidence*, and used it to prove evidence of absence. We looked for evidence, and couldn't find any.
   This argument has a different structure. First, it just says "we don't know". We don't know if people tried to find out whether the general was a traitor.
   Second, the stimulus has a clear conditional link between life and evidence of life. If there were life, there'd be evidence.
   This argument has shown no conditional link between being a spy and being a traitor.
B. This doesn't match the structure. The conclusion is "unlikely", whereas the stimulus said there has "never" been life on the moon.
   Further, in the stimulus people actually looked for evidence of life. Whereas this loser couldn't even be bothered to open his fridge to check for mayo.
C. This is a terrible argument, but it doesn't mirror the absence of evidence flaw.
   The flaw here is that the argument gave no evidence about what concerns voters. Unless they care about crime, Hendricks doesn't have a chance. The argument said what Hendricks wants, but not what voters want.
D. This is a bad argument, but the error is different. Here, finding signs of rodents is a *necessary* condition. The argument incorrectly takes it to be a sufficient condition.
E. **CORRECT.** This matches the absence of evidence error. The author has shown that we *haven't found* troop movements or a transfer of weapons. But that doesn't mean those things *don't exist.*

Question 10

QUESTION TYPE: Flawed Reasoning

CONCLUSION: There's a good argument that the defendant is not completely innocent.

REASONING: Why would the prosecutor have brought the case if the defendant was completely innocent?

ANALYSIS: This is a very bad argument. It relies entirely on the authority of the prosecutor.

The defendant has an alibi. There is much evidence in their favor. The jury agrees. So literally the only thing left is the prosecutor's initial decision to press charges. That's pure argument from authority.

———————————

A. This is a different flaw.
   Example of flaw: You have no evidence that there are people in that building. So the building must be empty.
B. This describes circular reasoning. That's almost never the correct answer, because it's very obvious.
   Example of flaw: The defendant must be guilty, because clearly they are guilty.
C. **CORRECT.** The prosecutor is the authority figure. The television host is relying on the prosecutor's authority despite the mass of evidence that the defendant is innocent.
D. This is a different flaw.
   Example of flaw: It was technically legal to take all the money out of the retirees' bank accounts even though the retirees wouldn't have wanted that.
   So therefore it was morally fine to do so.
E. The author didn't say this! Something can't be a flaw if it didn't happen.

Question 11

QUESTION TYPE: Method of Reasoning

CONCLUSION: The critics are wrong to say that S. N. Sauk's work lacks aesthetic merit.

REASONING: The critics have focussed on how Sauk's work differs from C. F. Providence's in terms of politics. However the critics have not shown that Sauk's work is any less well written than Providence's.

ANALYSIS: The critics are making an argument about beauty, but they use evidence relating to political views. So they're using irrelevant evidence.

_____

A. The literature professor didn't say the critics are wrong in their political conclusions. The professor was merely arguing that these conclusions weren't relevant.
B. Having aesthetic merit isn't the criteria. The criterion is "having *as much* aesthetic merit as Providence's work".
So the critics are wrong because they haven't shown Sauk's work has *less* aesthetic merit than Providence's.
There's a big difference between "has some merit" and "as good as Providence's"
C. The motivations of the critics aren't the issue. The problem is that the critics made a bad argument – their evidence is irrelevant to their conclusion!
D. This isn't the flaw. Even if the critics' claims are correct, they're still irrelevant to their conclusion.
E. **CORRECT.** The critics are arguing about the aesthetic value of Sauk's work, but their evidence is about the politics of Sauk's work. This is irrelevant evidence.

Question 12

QUESTION TYPE: Principle – Application

PRINCIPLE:

- Approve → Used elsewhere OR increase safety
- ~~Increase Safety~~ AND ~~Used elsewhere~~ → ~~Approve~~

APPLICATION: The inspector shouldn't approve the new welding process. We can't prove the process increases safety.

ANALYSIS: There were *two* conditions for rejecting a new process:

- Can't show the process increases safety.
- The process hasn't been used elsewhere for a year.

The application already shows the first reason. To prove the judgement correct, we just need to add the second reason.

_____

A. Problems weren't mentioned. Most complex processes will have *some* problems.
Stick to the items in the principle. If something isn't a sufficient or necessary condition listed in the principle, it's irrelevant.
B. **CORRECT.** This is the other sufficient condition for rejecting a process.
C. So? The condition is whether we can prove the new process *safer*. If the existing processes are not safer, that still could mean they are *as safe*. That would therefore be grounds for rejecting the new process.
D. This doesn't tell us whether the new process *has* been used elsewhere. That's the only important question.
E. This doesn't tell us anything. Was the process used in the other factory for more than a year? Was is safe?
We need a "no" to one of those questions for this to be the correct answer.

Question 13

QUESTION TYPE: Weaken

CONCLUSION: We shouldn't provide grad student teaching assistants with employee benefits.

REASONING: We're only giving jobs to grad students so that they can pay for their degrees. There are no other reasons.

ANALYSIS: On a weaken question, you're looking for a new fact that adds context to the argument, casting it into doubt.

The administrator has given just *one* reason not to pay teaching assistants more: the jobs are charity jobs intended to help them pay for degrees.

So the new fact will have to weaken this idea. As it happens, the right answer actually contradicts author on this point.

You may have heard you're not allowed to contradict a premise. Bollocks, of course you're allowed. It's just *rare*. Prep companies tell you not to do it because most people try to do it *on every question* and they choose answers that don't contradict anything. That's a mistake. But if an answer actually contradicts a premise, it's fine to pick.

A. *Of course* the administrator knows the extra costs. What kind of idiot would talk about an issue while ignorant of the facts?
   This doesn't mean they have an ulterior motive.
B. This doesn't affect the argument. It doesn't matter what pay adjuncts should receive. It only matters what pay teaching assistant should receive. This answer hasn't shown adjunct pay is relevant to teaching assistant pay.
C. **CORRECT.** This shows the administrator is wrong. There are other motives for hiring teaching assistants. In this case, the university wants to hire more of them to save money.
D. "Funding education" usually includes living expenses. So the higher-than-tuition stipends may still be entirely intended to fund education.
E. So? People don't earn money merely for working hard. This doesn't affect the administrator's claim that the lack of employee benefits is justified because the jobs are charity jobs.

Question 14

QUESTION TYPE: Flawed Parallel Reasoning

CONCLUSION: We'd have less air pollution if people moved from cities to rural areas.

REASONING: Most air pollution comes from large cities. If more people moved out of cities, cities would pollute less.

ANALYSIS: This is a terrible argument. The author hasn't shown that an individual person will pollute less in the countryside than in the city.

If people pollute the same no matter where they live, then moving people out of cities is just shuffling around pollution.

A. This isn't a bad argument, but it isn't the same flaw. The flaw here is that while Monique is likely to spend *more* on housing, that doesn't mean she'll spent *most* of her money on housing.
B. This argument is flawed, but it's a different flaw. This argument mistakes average properties for individual properties.
   It's possible that Karen's apartment is an extremely large apartment, and so most homes would be smaller than her family's apartment.
C. This makes a whole-to-part flaw. We only know that most farms switched to corn. That doesn't mean that *all* farms switched.
   The stimulus didn't make a whole-to-part flaw.
D. **CORRECT.** This makes the same flaw. The argument suggests that Javier should shuffle around his calories. But unless Javier actually eats *less* food, then he'll still eat the same number of calories under the new plan.
E. This answer matches the subject of the stimulus, but that's not necessary for an analogy. In fact, commonly the same subject is used merely to fool you into thinking an answer is relevant. This argument is flawed, but it's a different flaw – there's no shuffling around of pollution.
   The flaw is that while it sounds like public transit could *reduce* pollution, but we don't know that it could eliminate *most* pollution. We're not told if cars produce most pollution.

Question 15

QUESTION TYPE: Sufficient Assumption

CONCLUSION: The car buyers were wrong to say that safety was important to them.

REASONING: Ninety percent of car buyers said safety was important. Half of the car buyers looked at objective sources. The others half only looked at ads and marketing material.

ANALYSIS: We can conclude two things:

- At least 40% of car buyers only looked at promotional material.
- Promotional material is not objective.

We know the second point is true because the argument says half looked at objective material, and "the others" looked only at promotional material. So that material is not objective.

However, this doesn't let us conclude that these buyers didn't care about safety. We need to connect the evidence to the conclusion:

How to fill gap: Didn't consult objective material → Safety not important

Normally I would draw sufficient assumption questions. However this one was easier to reason out without drawings, apart from the single conditional I drew that connects things.

Note: You might think it's impossible to care about safety without consulting objective materials. But this is an unfounded assumption.

You might want to know, for example, that a car has airbags, seat-belts and antilock breaks. Promotional materials *are* a good source of information for that kind of knowledge. They may not be *optimal* for safety knowledge, but they do provide some information.

A. Who cares about the most important factor? Consumers weren't claiming that safety was the most important factor.

B. So? Just because advertising is *incomplete* doesn't mean the people using it don't care about safety.

You can care about safety while doing a poor job of investigating it.

C. So? "Do not necessarily" is weak language. It only lets us prove that it's possible that people were lying. But the conclusion is that people were *definitely 100% wrong* to say they cared about safety.

D. So? This still doesn't get to the central point. Consumers might reasonably believe they could care about safety without looking at objective materials.

For instance if consumers just want to know that a car has safety features like antilock breaks and airbags, they could learn that information purely from promotional materials.

E. **CORRECT.** This fills the gap. It takes what we know about some consumers, and lets us conclude they don't care about safety.

Cares about safety → consult objective material

~~consult objective material → cares about safety~~

Question 16

QUESTION TYPE: Flawed Reasoning

CONCLUSION: No planned locomotion → no central nervous system

REASONING: No central nervous system → no planned locomotion

ANALYSIS: This argument makes a classic flaw: incorrect reversal. That's when you reverse the conditions of an if/then statement. I.e. Taking "all cats have tails" to mean "This dog has a tail so it must be a cat".

Note that the first sentence of the stimulus is just context for why central nervous systems are needed for locomotion. It's not structurally relevant to the argument.

Note on B, C and E: Scientific questions often have nonsense answers. They take two terms from the argument, and reverse them or combine them in a new way. An answer can't be a flaw if the author didn't say it.

They're simply gibberish intended to bog you down. This is why it's important to prephrase answers. If you knew this argument made an incorrect reversal, you could quickly skip over these gibberish answers.

———————————

A. CORRECT. See the analysis above.
B. The argument didn't say this! This answer incorrectly reverses what the author said in the first sentence.
C. The author never mentioned biologically useful purposes.
D. This is a different flaw.
   Example of flaw: Our hands let us use computers, so hands must have evolved so that we can use computers.
E. The author didn't say this! This answer says that nervous systems lead to the ability to form internal representations (Nervous system → representation).
   But actually, *the author* said that nervous systems are a necessary condition for forming an internal representation (representation → nervous system)

Question 17

QUESTION TYPE: Necessary Assumption

CONCLUSION: Rockets need long and short nozzles for their ascents.

REASONING: At low altitudes, rockets need short nozzles. In the upper atmosphere, rockets need long nozzles.

ANALYSIS: This already sounds like a good argument. But, you know this is flawed. So how could this be wrong? Well, what if some rockets only make short ascents. Maybe some rockets never hit high altitudes. In which case they would only need short nozzles.

So the argument is assuming that every rocket goes high enough to hit the thin upper atmosphere.

(You may have thought that all rockets are space rockets. Nope. Some rockets, such as ICBMs, never leave the atmosphere. All missiles are rockets.)

A. It doesn't matter how difficult it is to equip nozzles. The argument is only about whether rockets *need* both nozzles.

B. **CORRECT.** If this isn't true, then not all rockets need long nozzles.
   Negation: Some rockets don't pass through the thin upper atmosphere.

C. The argument says rockets need both nozzles to be are *most effective*. But a rocket might be able to reach high altitudes even if it's not fully effective.
   Negation: Less than effective rockets can still reach high altitudes even with only short nozzles.

D. This is an absurd answer. Absurd answers are almost never correct. Rockets only have two types of nozzle, and air pressure changes constantly as you rise in the atmosphere. So it's impossible to match pressure exactly through ascent.
   Also, this answer talks about working effectively. The stimulus is about what's required to work *most effectively*. Those are two very different things.
   I worked effectively today, but I could have been far more effective.

E. This isn't necessary. The argument only said the engines need long and short nozzles. It's possible these could be on separate engines.
   Negation: A rocket can be most effective if it has zero engines with long and short, as long as there are some engines with long and some engines with short.

Question 18

QUESTION TYPE: Flawed Reasoning

CONCLUSION: Manufacturers of children's toys shouldn't overstate dangers on warning labels.

REASONING: Manufacturers should overstate dangers only if this reduces the chance of injuries.

Manufacturers overstate dangers in order to protect against lawsuits.

ANALYSIS: This argument mixes up the reasons for actions and the effects of actions.

Sure, manufacturers are only overstating dangers to protect themselves. However, it's possible that overstating dangers nonetheless has the *effect* of making toys safer. In which case overstatement is fine.

A. This is a different flaw. Reversing conditions will be pretty obvious when it happens.
   Example of flaw: You should overstate dangers only if it reduces injuries. So if you reduced injuries, you must have overstated the dangers.
B. The author is saying that it's *bad* to overstate dangers unless this reduces injuries. This claim can stand on its own.
   Regular warning don't have to be perfect in order for the author's claim to be true. Claims are rarely linked like this.
C. Unrepresentative sampling is a different flaw.
   Example of flaw: Billy the bonehead and Amber the arsonist both did dangerous things with our toys. So all children will do dangerous things with our toys.
D. The author didn't say this! The author said not to overstate dangers unless doing so reduces injuries.That implies that it *is* possible for a warning to reduce injuries, if manufacturers had different motives. So since this answer didn't happen, it can't be the flaw.
E. **CORRECT.** It's possible for actions to have multiple effects. Overstated labels could reduce the chance of lawsuits *but also* have the unintended effect of reducing injuries.

Question 19

QUESTION TYPE: Necessary Assumption

CONCLUSION: Tea boosted the immune systems of participants in the study.

REASONING: Compared to people who drank coffee, the immune systems of tea drinkers responded twice as fast.

ANALYSIS: This is a bad study: there's no control group. The conclusion compares tea drinkers to regular people, but the evidence only compares tree drinkers to coffee drinkers.

It's possible that coffee hurts immune systems. In which case tea may not actually help: it would only look good compared to coffee.

A. This doesn't matter. The argument was only comparing those who drank one liquid but not both.
   Negation: One person drank both coffee and tea. They weren't considered in the argument.
B. It doesn't matter if coffee has other health benefits. The argument is only talking about coffee and tea's effects on the immune system.
C. **CORRECT.** If coffee caused response time to double, then that means that tea had no impact. E.g.
   * Regular response time: 5s
   * Tea response time: 5s
   * Coffee response time: 10s
   Negation: Coffee caused immune system response time to double.
D. The author didn't say the study was about *regular* coffee and tea drinkers. Researchers could have given random people coffee and tea. Also, even if the study was about regular drinkers, the negation of this answer makes coffee drinkers *healthier,* so we would expect faster immune response. The fact that that didn't happen strengthens the argument.
   Negation: Regular coffee drinkers have healthier habits than tea drinkers do.
E. It doesn't matter if coffee and tea have some stuff in common, as long as they're not identical.
   Negation: Coffee and tea have one chemical in common, and 1,000 chemicals that are different.

Question 20

QUESTION TYPE: Role in Argument

CONCLUSION: Semiplaning monohulls will probably be profitable.

REASONING: Semiplaning monohulls are more expensive than regular ships. But they offer the same advantages over regular ships as jets do over regular airplanes: greater speed and reliability.

ANALYSIS: You're not supposed to be critical on role in argument questions. You just have to figure out what's going on in the argument.

Here you're being asked to explain why the author says that semiplane monohulls are more expensive. The author says this is a disadvantage of semiplane monohulls. The argument then uses an analogy to jet planes to show this disadvantage won't be decisive.

———————————

A. There *aren't* two analogies between semiplane monohulls and jets. Only one, comparing the attributes of jets and monohulls: both are more expensive, but also faster and more reliable. Stating that monohulls are more expensive is part of the same analogy.
Trust me, you'll know *two* analogies when you see it.
B. There's no analogy between semiplane monohulls and normal ships. The argument just points out a *difference* between them: semiplane monohulls are more expensive, but faster.
C. Actually, saying that semiplane monohulls are more expensive works *against* the conclusion. The author concludes that semiplane monohulls will be profitable *despite* their cost.
D. **CORRECT.** This matches. The high price of semiplane monohulls is an argument against them. However, the jet plane analogy shows that monohulls are likely to succeed nonetheless.
E. Nonsense. The statement in question draws a distinction on *one* characteristic: price.
This answer talks about characteristics, plural. The part about the conclusion is wrong too – the conclusion wasn't about airplane distinctions. The conclusion was that semiplane monohulls will probably succeed.

Question 21

QUESTION TYPE: Strengthen

CONCLUSION: Maté probably originated in Paraguay.

REASONING: Maté is used more widely in Paraguay than elsewhere, and there are more varieties of it there too.

ANALYSIS: This isn't a very good argument. To strengthen it, we can say that Maté probably originated in the area where it has the most varieties or where it is used more widely.

———————————

A. In use "for a very long time" isn't the right comparison. We want to find where Maté *originated*.
B. Who cares what Paraguayans *believe?* We want to know what's true, not what's popularly believed. Belief can't establish fact.
C. The argument doesn't say that the best maté shows where maté originated. Also, this answer is only about belief, not fact.
D. This doesn't help us prove which place *in* South America maté originated. Much of South America drinks maté.
E. **CORRECT.** This supports the argument. Maté is more widely used in Paraguay than anywhere else. So this answer suggests that maté may have originated in Paraguay.

Question 22

QUESTION TYPE: Weaken – Exception

CONCLUSION: Opponents say the 10% decline in average family income is the political party's fault.

REASONING: No reasoning is given.

ANALYSIS: There was a 10% inflation-adjusted decline in family income from 1996-2004.

No reasoning is given. And this is an "exception" question, so there are many ways to weaken the opposition's claim. Just look at the answers with an open mind.

A. **CORRECT.** This isn's significant. It's probable there were ups and downs in individual years. The main point is that over the whole period from 1996-2004, incomes fells 10%.
B. This suggests the decline isn't the party's fault or even a problem. For instance, maybe some families decided to spend more time traveling or taking care of their children. This leads to less income, but there's nothing wrong with that.
C. This shows the party wasn't responsible. The decline was due to international trouble.
D. This suggests the decline is due to demographic change, not any bad policy.
E. This shows the causes of the decline occurred before the party took power.

Question 23

QUESTION TYPE: Necessary Assumption

CONCLUSION: Amateur gardeners using phases of the moon are less likely to lose crops to frost.

REASONING: Other amateur gardeners often plant in the first warm spell of spring. This leads to problems if there is frost.

ANALYSIS: The argument hasn't shown that planting according to the phases of the moon avoids early planting and frost problems.

A. **CORRECT.** If this isn't true, then moon-phase planters will be just as vulnerable to frost.
   Negation: Moon-phase planters will plant just as early as those who plant at the first warm spell.
B. It isn't necessary that the moon *affects* frost. It only matters if the phases of the moon let gardeners *avoid planting* before a frost.
C. Different types of plants aren't the crucial point. Whether or not plants get hit by frost is the key point.
   Negation: Farmers who plant according to the phases of the moon use different plants, but these plants are equally vulnerable to frost.
D. This has no impact on the argument. In fact the negation even seems to strengthen the idea that moon-planting will help, despite our lack of understanding of why it works.
   Negation: Amateur gardeners can improve even if they don't know why their methods work.
E. So? The argument wasn't comparing amateur gardeners to professional gardeners.

Question 24

QUESTION TYPE: Most Strongly Supported

FACTS:

1. About 70% of tourism industry profit in developing countries goes to foreign owners.
2. The more established the tourist destination, the more profits go abroad, in general.
3. Tourists can avoid this transfer abroad by dealing directly with locals.

ANALYSIS: I couldn't think of how to combine anything. When that happens, I just make sure I know the facts clearly before moving on.

The more you can memorize a list like the one I wrote above, the easier the answers will be. I at least skim over a MSS question again before I check the answers. This lets me retain information better and go through the answers faster.

A. The question doesn't tell us what people *should* do. It only says what tourists *can* do. Maybe it doesn't matter if profits stay in a country or go abroad.
B. **CORRECT.** This is very well supported. In the average country, 70% of revenues go to foreign owners. And in developed tourist markets, even more tends to go to foreign owners.
   So mathematically, at least some of the countries with the most developed tourist industries send most (51%+) of their profits to foreign owners.
C. The stimulus said that people *could* get services from locals. It didn't say that they actually do.
D. Nonsense. The author said that tourism profits tend to go abroad. But that doesn't mean the country gets poorer. In fact unless 100% of profits go abroad, tourism will probably make a country richer.
E. Hard to say. Some of locals' spending might end up in the hands of foreign owners.
   For instance, imagine a local takes a bus owned by a tourist company in order to go to a tourist location where they'll sell their native crafts. The local gets the money from the sale of the crafts, but they still gave some money to the foreign owners.

Question 25

QUESTION TYPE: Necessary Assumption

CONCLUSION: We can't know if the recent decline of certain amphibian species is due to pollution.

REASONING: Weather variations can also cause changes in most amphibian populations. Amphibian populations decreased quite a bit recently.

ANALYSIS: This seems like a good argument. But there is a flaw of course – otherwise this wouldn't be a necessary assumption question.

Weather causes variations, but there are surely limits. If amphibian populations declined far past normal changes caused by weather, then we could suspect pollution.

The other possible flaw is that the argument only said that *most* amphibian species can decline due to weather. If there are some amphibian species that *don't* decline from weather, then we could be surer that those species declined from pollution.

Note that the wrong answers make odd linkages between elements from the stimulus. It's very, very rare for this type of answer to be right. Mostly they are used to slow you down, because the brain interprets familiar concepts as possible answers.

A. **CORRECT.** Negate this and the argument falls apart.
   Negation: The amphibian species that declined are among those species whose populations do not change much with the weather.
B. The argument is *stronger* if this isn't true.
   Negation: Declines due to weather variation are always as large as those attributed to pollution.
C. This is hardly necessary. It's possible industrial pollution caused most of the decline but weather contributed a bit. Real world causes are rarely exclusive.
   Negation: It's possible that both pollution and weather had some contribution to the decline.
D. The argument is talking about the causes of the past decline, not what will happen in the future.
E. Why would this be necessary? The scientists made no link between pollution and weather.

Section IV – Logic Games
Game 1 – Finance and Graphics Bonuses
Questions 1–6

Setup

This game combines linear and grouping elements. On recent LSATs the LSAC has been making more unique, unusual games. I do not believe these games are *harder* than past games. I merely think they are *different*.

For new LSATs, you should not focus on memorizing game "types". The people who are the very best at logic games do not decide how to approach a game based on type. They just focus on what the rules say.

Your best approach is to work through past games to mastery, so that you know how different rules work and what constraints within games will have large effects. This will let you quickly and correctly solve unusual games, like this one.

Also, don't use explanations *too* much, including mine. To beat these unusual games you need to practice figuring out games on your own, before checking outside resources. You can learn a lot by repeating games *before* checking explanations.

This game splits seven employees across two groups: Finance and Graphics. It's best to represent the two groups like this:

F:

G:

One key to games is having all of the elements present so you can use them. It's important that elements be close to each other. If you have to search to find things, you are taking away short-term working memory that could be spent on solving the question.

In this case, I initially made my list of variables *directly above* each diagram:

K, P, <u>L</u>, <u>M</u>
F:

V, Z, <u>X</u>
G:

I've also underlined L, M and X to cover the final two rules:

- Lopez, Meng and Xavier are highly effective.
- The highly effective people have a higher bonus than the others.

That covers rules two and three. Note that I don't always draw the rules in order. I want a clear, logical diagram. I don't know how best to draw things until I've read all the rules. I draw them in the order that makes the most sense, once I've read them all.

Ok, so now only the first rule is left: no one in Graphics gets a $1,000 bonus. That means graphics employees can only get $3,000 or $5,000 bonuses.

We know that Xavier has a higher bonus than Vaughan and Zane, thanks to rules two and three combined. So that means Xavier has a $5,000 bonus, while the other two only earn $3,000:

K, P, <u>L</u>, <u>M</u>
F:

G: V, Z   X
      3   5

So *everything* is determined for the graphics department.

The finance department, on the other hand, is more flexible. We know that L and M are higher than K and P. But that's *all* we know.

If I've counted correctly, there are *twenty* ways we could arrange the bonuses in the finance department. It's inefficient to draw them all.

So the graphics department is fully determined, and already on the diagram. You only need to remember *two* things:

- The bonuses are $1,000, $3,000 and $5,000
- L and M have higher bonuses than K and P

The questions will do the rest. A question will give you something like "Lopez and Meng get different bonuses". That immediately cuts the possibilities down to one diagram: K and P have $1000, and one of L/M gets $3000 and the other gets $5000. It's much simpler to wait for the questions to narrow things down before you spend brainpower figuring out possibilities.

On the setup, stick to what *must* be true.

Main Diagram

F : K, P, <u>L</u> , <u>M</u>

G : V, Z X
    3   5

The graphics department is fully determined. The lines under L and M indicate that they have higher bonuses than K and P.

The possibilities for the finance department are $1000, $3000 or $5000.

Question 1

For acceptable order questions, go through the rules and use them to eliminate answers one by one.

Note that I use the rules themselves. I don't use my diagrams for these questions. Reading the rules again for this question will help you memorize them, and it's also more efficient. Note that this game is a minor exception: rules 2 and 3 only have an effect when you consider them together.

Rule 1 eliminates **B** and **E.** No one in the graphics department is allowed to have a $1,000 bonus. But in **B,** Zane has a $1,000 bonus. In **E,** Vaughan has a $1,000 bonus.

Rules 2 + 3 eliminate **A** and **D.** It's impossible to consider rules 2 + 3 separately, as they only have an effect jointly.

In **A,** Xavier should have a higher bonus than the other two. In **D,** Meng should have a higher bonus than Kimura.

C is **CORRECT.** It violates no rules.

Question 2

Question two gives us a new rule: Lopez and Meng get different bonuses.

We already knew from the setup that Lopez and Meng have higher bonuses than Kimura and Peterson (rules 2 + 3). That's because L and M are highly effective, and highly effective people get higher bonuses.

So to give L and M higher bonuses and also *different* bonuses, we need to give P and K $1,000. Then one of L/M will get $3,000 and the other will get $5,000.

```
                 ⌒
F:  K , P    L    M
     1       3    5
G:  V , Z    X
       3     5
```

The line above L and M shows that they are interchangeable.

This is a "could be true" question.
The above diagram shows that **B is CORRECT:** Lopez could receive a $3,000 bonus (or a $5,000 bonus).

All of the other answers are impossible.

Question 3

This question says only one employee gets a $1,000 bonus. Here's what we can conclude about the $1,000 bonus:

- Rule 1 says that none of the graphic employees can receive a $1,000 bonus.
- So a finance employee receives the bonus. It won't be Lopez or Meng, because they are rated Highly Effective.

Therefore we can conclude that one of Kimura and Peterson has $1,000 and the other has $3,000 (because the question says only *one* person has $1,000):

```
         ⌒
F:  K    P    L , M
    1    3      5
G:  V , Z    X
      3      5
```

Both Lopez and Meng receive $5,000 because they are rated Highly Effective and so they need higher bonuses than the others (rules 2 and 3).

Therefore, **A is CORRECT.** Meng must receive $5,000.

In the diagram, the line above K and P shows that they are interchangeable. That's why **B-D** are wrong. One of them gets $1,000, the other $3,000, but it doesn't matter *which* one of them gets $1,000 or $3,000.

If any of that description is confusing, read over the steps one by one and draw them. There's no simpler way to approach this question. Logic games depend on taking each deduction and combining it with the rules to form a new deduction. Step by step.

59

Question 4

I solved this question by looking at the main diagram, and trying to prove answers false. Since this is a "must be true" question, any answer that could be false isn't the right answer. Here's the main diagram:

F: K, P, L̲ , M̲

G: V, Z   X
      3   5

Since this is an explanation, I'm going to draw diagrams disproving **A-D.** But you should know that on my own test I *did not* make drawings for this question. I found it easiest to visualize possibilities in my head using the diagram. For example, I can look at that diagram and imagine K and P having $1000 and L/M having some combination of $3000/$5000. Or K and P having $1000/$3000 and L/M having $5000, etc.

However, if you make mistakes visualizing, then you should definitely draw diagrams.

This diagram proves that **A** and **C** could be false. No employees have a $1000 bonus, and four employees have a $3000 bonus.:

F: K, P   L,M
        3   5

G: V, Z   X
      3   5

This diagram proves that **B** could be false. Only two employees have a $3000 bonus.:

F: K, P   L,M
        1   5

G: V, Z   X
      3   5

This diagram proves that **D** could be false. Only Xavier has a $5,000 bonus:

F: K, P   L,M
        1   3

G: V, Z   X
      3   5

E is **CORRECT.** Highly effective employees must have the highest bonuses, so they're the only ones who can have $5,000. And there are only three highly effective employees: Xavier, Lopez and Meng.

Note that while you can prove **E** right by logic, I didn't find it easy to predict in advance that it would be right. So I disproved the other answers by quickly visualizing that they could be false.

However, if visualization is slow, it may be optimal for you to focus on answers that seem to have the most restrictions. For instance, you might notice that $5000 is restricted because only highly effective people can have $5000.

Question 5

This question asks what happens if precisely two employees receive $5,000 bonuses.

We already know that in the graphics department, only Xavier receives a $5,000 bonus.

That means that exactly *one* Finance employee will get the second $5,000 bonus. And it will have to be a highly rated employee, since they receive the highest bonuses.

So one of Lopez and Meng will get $5,000. The other will get $3,000, because highly effective employees need higher bonuses. The non-highly rated employees will both get $1000:

F: K, P   L‿‿‿M
        1   3   5

G: V, Z   X
      3   5

The arc above L and M shows that they are interchangeable. This interchangeability disproves **A, B** and **C,** since interchangeable variables can't be right for "must be true" questions.

D is **CORRECT.** Peterson must receive a $1000 bonus.

E must be false and is therefore wrong. Peterson receives $1,000, not $3,000.

This diagram shows that **D** and **E** are possible:

F: K, P   L, M
    1   3

G: V, Z   X
    3   5

There are two $1,000 bonuses and only one $5,000 bonus.

There are also two $3,000 bonuses and only one $5,000 bonus.

B is **CORRECT.** Only K and P can have $1,000 bonuses, because they are lower rated than L and M. And rule 1 bans anyone in the graphics department from having a $1,000 bonus.

We saw in the setup that V and Z have $3,000. That's because they must have less than X, since X is highly rated. So there are at least two $3,000 bonuses, and at most two $1,000 bonuses.

Main diagram:

F: K, P, L̲, M̲

G: V, Z   X
    3   5

K and P are the only ones that can have $1,000. (The lines under L and M indicate that L and M are highly rated and therefore have higher bonuses).

Question 6

This is a must be false question. Just like question 4, I used my main diagram to visualize scenarios. If a scenario is possible, then the answer is wrong:

F: K, P, L̲, M̲

G: V, Z   X
    3   5

If you have trouble with visualization, it's better to draw diagrams. I'm going to draw some here for the purposes of clarity in this explanation. But note that I did this in my head in timed conditions, because I was sure I could do it faster yet correctly that way:

This diagram shows that **A** is possible:

F: K, P   L, M
    1   5

G: V, Z   X
    3   5

There are two $1,000 bonuses and two $3,000 bonuses.

This diagram shows that **C** is possible:

F: K, P   L   M
    1   3   5

G: V, Z   X
    3   5

There are two $1,000 bonuses and two $5,000 bonuses.

Game 2 – Trees in lots
Questions 7–11

Setup

This is a grouping game. We have to place seven trees in three lots.

From experience with similar games, it's best to set this game up vertically:

1 ___

2 ___

3 ___

Next, read over all the rules. You shouldn't just blindly draw the rules in order. Some rules are easier to draw than others, because they can go directly on the diagram. Draw these first.

Rules 3, 4 and 5 can go directly on the diagram:

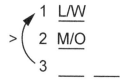

A couple notes on the symbols:

Technically, L/W and M/O are exclusive. You can't have both. I know I'll remember that because I've seen similar rules. If you aren't certain you'll remember, it's best to make a separate note. Maybe "L̶/̶W̶" to the left of lot one, for example.

Lot three has at least two trees, because it has more than lot 1. The arrow + greater than sign is a second reminder of this rule.

This final rule is incredibly important. In *every* scenario you make you must check if lot three has more than lot one. And in some cases, the final rule determines the distribution.

For example, some questions place exactly three trees in lot two. This means that lot 1 has one tree and lot 3 has three trees – that's the only way to divide the trees between those two lots and still obey the final rule.

The other two rules can't be drawn directly, so you should put them in a numbered list:

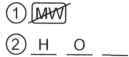

The circled P and S means that those two variables have no rules. The "H O ___" means that the hickory and the oak are in a lot together with one other tree.

I couldn't make any deductions that I could draw. However, it's important to consider numerical distributions.

We have seven trees. At least one is in lot 2. That leaves six trees to divide between lot 1 and 3. And lot 3 needs more than lot 1.

That means we *can't* put three trees in lot 1, because then there would only be three trees to put in lot 3.

So lot one has, at most, two trees. I didn't write this down because it's fairly straightforward if you remember the final rule. But it you sometimes make mistakes with numerical distributions, you should write this deduction down.

Likewise, it's important to consider where you could place the hickory, oak and 3rd tree (rule one). They could only go in lots 2 or 3, because lot 1 can't have three trees.

Main Diagram

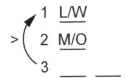

It's important to consider numerical distributions. To obey the final rule, lot three needs at least two trees. Lot one can have *at most* two trees.

Rules:

Question 7

For acceptable order questions, go through the rules and use them to eliminate answers one by one.

Note that I use the rules themselves. I don't use my diagrams for these questions. Reading the rules again for this question will help you memorize them, and it's also more efficient.

Rule 1 eliminates **A.** The hickory and the oak must go together with one other tree. In **A** they are alone.

Rule 2 eliminates no answers.

Rule 3 eliminates **C.** Lot one needs the larch or the walnut. Instead it has only the maple.

Rule 4 eliminates **E.** Lot two needs either the walnut or the larch. In **E** it has only the plum and the sycamore.

Rule 5 eliminates **B.** Lot three is supposed to have more trees than lot one.

D is **CORRECT.** It violates no rules.

Question 8

This question says that the hickory is planted on lot 2. Whenever a question gives you a new rule, you should draw it and then combine the new rule with the existing rules.

Rule 1 mentions the hickory. The hickory must go with the oak and *exactly* one other tree:

```
   1   L/W
>(  2   H    O   ___|
   3   ___  ___
```

The vertical line by lot 2 shows that it's full.

Next, consider the other rules. We know that lot three needs more trees than lot one. There are only four trees left. So we need to place three trees in lot three and one tree in lot one:

```
   1   L/W |
>(  2   H    O   ___|
   3   ___  ___  ___|
```

Next consider the other rules. They are:

- Maple and Walnut aren't together.
- *One* of L/W goes in lot one.
- *One* of M/O goes in lot two.

The third one is affected by our setup. The oak is already in lot two, so the maple *can't* go there. And the maple can't go in lot one, because one of L/W must go there.

So the maple must go in lot three:

```
   1   L/W
>(  2   H    O   ___|
   3   M   ___  ___|
```

Whenever you make an extended deduction like this, you should check the answers, because this type of deduction usually solves the question instantly.

B is **CORRECT.** The maple must go in lot three. **A, C** and **D** could be true but don't have to be. **E** must be false.

Question 9

This question asks for all the trees that could go in lot one. You should first eliminate answers. There are two good ways to eliminate:

- Up front logic
- The correct answer to the first question

Logic: in the setup, I described how lot one can only have two trees at most, thanks to rule 5. Lot three needs to have more trees than lot one.

So the hickory and the oak can't go in lot one, since rule 1 says that the hickory, the oak and one other tree go together. That's three trees.

So any answer with H or O is wrong. **A** and **B** are wrong since they contain the hickory.

First question: On almost all logic games the first question is easy to get right with certainty. So you can use this as a correct hypothetical.

The right answer to question seven places the sycamore and the walnut in lot one. Therefore, **D** is wrong because it doesn't include the sycamore.

Now we are left to choose between **C** and **E.** The two answers are the same, except that **C** contains the larch and **E** doesn't.

You might be tempted to just choose **C,** since rule 3 says that the larch or the walnut goes in lot one (but not both).

That's a bad habit. On past games it's been the case that a variable mentioned as a possibility for a lot actually can't go in the lot. So before choosing **C** it's best to make a quick hypothetical proving that the larch can indeed go in lot one. Like this:

```
   1   L
>(  2   H    O   W
   3   M    P   S
```

So **C** is **CORRECT.** Making a diagram like that should only take ~7 seconds. If it takes longer, practice! It's a learnable skill.

Question 10

This question places the walnut on lot three. When that happens, you should draw the hypothetical and combine it with the existing rules:

```
        1   L
        2  M/O
  M     3   W    ___
```

Rule two says that the maple is not with the walnut, so we can draw M̶ beside lot three. And rule three says that the larch or the walnut is in lot 1. Since the walnut is in lot 3, we must place the larch in lot 1.

Next let's consider the fourth rule: the maple or the oak is planted in lot 2.

If we plant the oak there, then we need to plant the hickory, the oak, and one other tree. And the other tree can't be the maple, because the oak and the maple can't go together in lot 2 (rule four):

```
          1   L
  M̶      2   H    O    ___ |
  M̶      3   W    ___
```

That means the maple would have to go in lot 1:

```
          1   L    M
  M̶      2   H    O    ___ |
  M̶      3   W    ___
```

But this diagram *doesn't work.* We have distributed spaces for seven trees, but lot 3 doesn't have more than lot 1. This violates rule five.

So the hickory and the oak can't go in lot 2. And thanks to rule five, there's no space for them in lot 1 either. So we must place them in lot 3:

```
        1   L
  >(    2   M
        3   W    H    O  |
```

That also means we must place the maple in lot 2 in order to obey the fourth rule (maple or oak in lot 2).

Now we have the plum and the sycamore left to place. Lot 3 is full (rule 1) and so they can go in lots 1 or 2. Of course, at least one must go in lot 2, because lot one needs fewer trees than lot 3 (rule 5).

This is a could be true question, so either the plum or the sycamore in lot 1 or 2 will be the right answer.

A is CORRECT. The diagram above shows that all the other answers are impossible.

Note that these diagrams take a lot of words to *explain*, but they shouldn't take that long to *draw.* This type of question can be solved fairly quickly, since your brain works without words. If these deductions took you a long time, then practice repeating them in order to learn to do the process faster.

Question 11

This question asks which tree will completely determine the order, if you place it in lot 2.

You should think logically about what's restricted before looking at the answers. We know that lot 2 *needs* one of the maple or the oak. So placing a variable that *isn't* the maple or the oak is more restrictive.

Next, we know two other things about lot 2:

- If we place the oak, then H and one other tree must also go there. (rule 1)
- If we place the maple, then the walnut can't go there. (rule 2)

So walnut and hickory are special, because they interact with other variables. And hickory isn't in the answers.

Let's try the walnut. If we plant W, then we can't plant the maple and we must plant the oak. Having the oak forces the hickory to go in lot 2 as well (rule 1):

```
      1 __
 M    2  W   H   O |
      3  __  __
```

Next we must obey rule 5. Lot three needs more trees than lot one. The only way to do this is to put one tree in lot 1 and three trees in lot 3:

```
      1 __ |
 M    2  W   H   O |
      3  __  __  __|
```

Next, rule three says that the larch or the walnut has to be in lot 1. Since the walnut is in lot 2, we must place the larch in lot 1:

```
      1  L  |
 M    2  W   H   O |
      3  __  __  __
```

Only M, S and P are left to place. Only lot three has space, so they must go there:

```
       1  L  |
   >(  2  W   H   O |
       3  M   S   P |
```

This diagram obeys all the rules, and it's the only possible diagram if we put the walnut in lot 2. So **A** is **CORRECT.**

On question like this, you could in theory test each of the answers to check that there are indeed multiple possibilities. But that would take a long time. If you're sure about the rules, you can be confident about choosing **A.**

However, it is possible to do some elimination. **B** and **C** are wrong because the sycamore and the plum are interchangeable. Both answers can't be right.

And the right answer to the first question eliminates **D** and **E.** That answer places both the larch and the maple in lot 2. The sycamore and the plum are in lots 1 and 3 respectively. Those two variables are interchangeable, so they could switch.

Thus even when the larch and the maple are both in lot 2 the order is not completely determined, and **D** and **E** are wrong.

It wasn't necessary to disprove answers **B-E,** but it also didn't take that long. The LSAT often has shortcuts like the ones I mentioned. If you're not completely sure, I'd eliminate the answers.

And for most questions I do check all the answers. The only reason I advocated skipping it here is that it could potentially take a long time to conclusively disprove answers **B-D.** The only reason it didn't is because the LSAC gave shortcuts.

Game 3 – Librarians (two on Saturday)
Questions 12–18

Setup

This is a sequencing game. It has a slight twist in that two librarians are on Saturday. Otherwise, it's exactly like pure sequencing games.

On these games, the optimal strategy is to combine all the rules into a large diagram. The only other difference on this game is that the final rule splits the game into two diagrams.

On this type of game the optimal strategy is to just draw the rules one by one and grow the diagram:

Rule 1:

H—L

Rule 2:

H—L
 \
  G
 /
M

Rule 3:

H—L
 \
  G
 /
M
/
F
 \
  K

Rule 4:

H—L
 \
  G
 /
M
/
F
 \
  K—Z

Rule 5 is the only tricky rule. It says that *either* L is before F, *or* L is on Saturday. So on the existing diagram we can just give L an "s" subscript to show it's on Saturday if it's after F:

H—L$_s$
 \
  G
 /
M
/
F
 \
  K—Z

Note that, *without* this rule, L could have been before F. L is after H, but H isn't connected to F. So we could have put both H and L before or after F. Even now, we can still put H before F.

So, *technically* we should draw a line from F to L to show that F is before L. However, for me that makes the diagram more confusing. Personally I have no trouble remembering that in this diagram, H could be before or after F (even first!) but L must be on Saturday.

For the second diagram, draw everything else in the same order but place H and L before F:

H—L—F—M—G
        \
         K—Z

That covers all possibilities. The rest is just reading the diagrams correctly. Remember, two librarians have a relationship *only if* lines connect them from left to right.

For instance, in the second diagram, we know *nothing* about the order or Z and M. Either could go before the other. Those two variables have no lines connecting them, so we have no idea which order they go in. The fact that Z is drawn to the right of M doesn't mean anything – it's the lines that matter.

On individual questions, I drew a diagram like this. But there's nothing you can put in it for now:

$$\overline{}$$

| $\overline{\text{M}}$ | $\overline{\text{T}}$ | $\overline{\text{W}}$ | $\overline{\text{Th}}$ | $\overline{\text{F}}$ | $\overline{\text{S}}$ |

Note that on my own page, I left off the days of the week. For me it's easy to see which day is which, because I've previously drawn many games that use the days of the week. And it's faster and smaller to draw diagrams without the days. I recommend you try it. I only drew them here in this explanation for clarity.

Main Diagram

F before L, L on Saturday:

```
   H—L_S
      \
       G
      /
    M
   /
  F
   \
    K—Z
```

L before F:

```
H—L—F—M—G
       \
        K—Z
```

Main Diagram:

$$\overline{}$$

| $\overline{\text{M}}$ | $\overline{\text{T}}$ | $\overline{\text{W}}$ | $\overline{\text{Th}}$ | $\overline{\text{F}}$ | $\overline{\text{S}}$ |

Note that on my own page I left off the days of the week. It's faster and small to draw without them, and I have no problem knowing which day is which. We all use weekly calendars often enough to have an intuition for that.

Question 12

For acceptable order questions, go through the rules and use them to eliminate answers one by one.

Note that I use the rules themselves. I don't use my diagrams for these questions. Reading the rules again for this question will help you memorize them, and it's also more efficient.

Rule 1 eliminates **E.** Hill needs to be earlier than Leung.

Rule 2 eliminates no answers.

Rule 3 eliminates **C.** Flynn must be earlier than Kitson and Moore.

Rule 4 eliminates **D.** Kitson must be earlier than Zahn.

Rule 5 eliminates **B.** Leung has to be earlier than Flynn, unless Leung is on Saturday. Here Leung is on Thursday.

A is **CORRECT.** It violates no rules.

68

Question 13

This question asks who can't be on Tuesday. Tuesday is the second day. To solve this type of question, just look at who needs to have two or more people in front of them.

Zahn and Gomez each have two people in front of them, so they can't go Tuesday. Either one could be the answer.

Since only Zahn is in the answers, **E is CORRECT.**

Question 14

This question places Kitson in front of Moore. There are two approaches. One would be redrawing both diagrams to account for this modification. The other would be looking at the diagrams, and visualizing K in front of M.

Either approach is fine. Personally I visualize, because I am good at visualization. If you find drawings clearer, here are the two modified drawings that place Kitson in front of Moore.

The scenarios are split according to the final rule (L on Saturday or L before F):

$$H - L_S$$
$$F - K - M - G$$
$$Z$$

$$H - L - F - K - M - G$$
$$Z$$

It took me about 10 seconds to draw those. It shouldn't be an agonizing decision. Either do it or don't. Time spent staring at the page wondering what to do is time you could have been visualizing or drawing. Logic games are about action, not thought.

From the diagrams, it's clear that **B is CORRECT.** Gomez can now no longer be in front of Kitson.

All of the other answers are possible in at least one of the diagrams. Remember that if variables don't have a line between them, we know *nothing*. So in the first diagram, for instance, Hill could be first.

All we know about Hill is that it's before L and G. In the first diagram there's a wide range of places H could go.

The same applies to Zahn. Zahn has quite a few options for placement, especially in the first diagram. *All* we know there is that Z is after F and K. They could be before or after anyone else.

Question 15

This question places Zahn on Thursday. You should draw that:

$$\underline{}\ \underline{}\ \underline{}\ \underset{\text{Th}}{\underline{\text{Z}}}\ \overline{\underline{}}\ \underline{}$$
M   T   W   Th   F   S

We need three variables after Zahn. This restricts our options. In the second scenario (L before F), only Moore and Gomez can go after Zahn:

$$\text{H}-\text{L}-\text{F}\overset{\displaystyle -\text{M}-\text{G}}{\underset{\displaystyle \searrow \text{K}-\text{Z}}{}}$$

So scenario 2 doesn't work. Looks like we're working with scenario 1:

$$\begin{array}{l} \text{H}-\text{L}_\text{S} \\ \quad\searrow \text{G} \\ \quad\nearrow \\ \text{M} \\ \nearrow \\ \text{F} \\ \quad\searrow \\ \quad\quad \text{K}-\text{Z} \end{array}$$

Here, H, M, L and G can go after Z. In fact, thanks to the final rule, L is on Saturday. And G has to go after H and M, so G is on Saturday too (because there's no one else left to go after G):

$$\underline{}\ \underline{}\ \underline{}\ \underset{\text{Th}}{\underline{\text{Z}}}\ \underline{}\ \underset{\text{S}}{\overset{\text{G}}{\underline{\text{L}}}}$$
M   T   W   Th   F   S

Once you make some major deductions like this, you should check the answers to see if you've already solved the question. It turns out I've actually already done more work than I needed to.

A is CORRECT. Leung is on Saturday, so Flynn is definitely before Leung.

We could have deduced this earlier merely from the fact that we knew we were working in scenario 1. However it's not a terrible idea to make the diagram with G and L on Saturday, because the answer also could also have said something like "Moore is earlier than Gomez" and that would have been the correct answer.

Question 16

This question places Moore on Tuesday. Your first step should be to draw that and combine it with existing rules.

We know that F is earlier than M (rule 3), so we can draw that:

$$\underset{\text{M}}{\underline{\text{F}}}\ \underset{\text{T}}{\underline{\text{M}}}\ \underline{}\ \underline{}\ \overline{\underline{}}\ \underline{}$$
M   T   W   Th   F   S

Rule five says that if F is earlier than L, then L is on Saturday. F is definitely earlier since F is first. So L is on Saturday:

$$\underset{\text{M}}{\underline{\text{F}}}\ \underset{\text{T}}{\underline{\text{M}}}\ \underline{}\ \underline{}\ \underline{}\ \underset{\text{S}}{\overset{}{\underline{\text{L}}}}$$
M   T   W   Th   F   S

This solves the question. **C is CORRECT.**

No need to consider the other answers, if you are sure your deductions are right. Also note that Hill, Kitson and Zahn all have considerable flexibility in how they are placed, making the other answers extremely unlikely to be correct.

Question 17

This question places Flynn earlier than Hill. This automatically put us in scenario 1, since scenario 2 has Hill before Flynn:

Scenario 1:

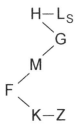

We can conclude two things:

Leung is on Saturday, due to rule 5.

Flynn is first. In scenario 1, H is the only librarian who could go before F. But this question places H after F.

Here's a diagram of what we know:

$$\overline{\underset{M}{F} \quad \underset{T}{\_} \quad \underset{W}{\_} \quad \underset{Th}{\_} \quad \underset{F}{\_} \quad \underset{S}{\overline{L}}}$$

Once you make deductions like these, you should check if they solve the question.

D is CORRECT. Moore is earlier than Gomez, and therefore not on Saturday. Therefore, Moore is also earlier than Leung. (Note: only Gomez or Zahn could have gone with Leung on Saturday).

All of the wrong answers involve H, K, M and Z. These librarians are incredibly flexible and can all go before and after one another (except K, who is before Z). So they are highly unlikely to be the basis for must be true answers when used in combination.

Question 18

This is a rule substitution question. Everyone hates them, but they're not that hard. They're just new, and therefore unfamiliar.

The rule in this case is: F is before K and M. You're looking for something that replicates all of the *effects* of the rule. So look at what we know about F.

- It's earlier than M, K, Z and G
- Only H and L could go before F

Just by phrasing the effects of the rule on F, we solve the question. **C is CORRECT.** It matches the second observation above.

If only H and L can go before F, then logically K, M, Z and G will all have to go after F. So this new rule leaves us with *exactly* the same possibilities for F, M and K as before.

A is just silly. It would let F be on Wednesday, but after both M and K.

B would allow F to go *last* if we placed H on Monday. That's very wrong.

D and **E** are both similar answers. They link F with the variables after M and K (G and Z). These answers don't work because they allow M and K to go before F, respectively.

Game 4 – Newsletter features and graphics
Questions 19–23

Setup

This game is fairly unique. I couldn't say what type to call it. It's sort of linear. Truth is, game type doesn't matter much. The main thing on any game is understanding the effect of the rules and how they interact, and knowing a game's "type" has nothing to do with that.

So in this game we have four features: finance, industry, marketing and technology. Features are interesting. They can span multiple slots. The game doesn't set a max number of slots. If there were no other rules, this would be an allowable setup:

```
1  F \
2  F  \
3  F   )
4  F  /
5  F /
```

That's a single finance feature filling all five slots. The arc to the right indicates that it's a single large feature.

This isn't an allowable combination because there *are* other rules. But I'm drawing it to show that there are no natural limits on the size of a feature.

In the setup, it says there at least three features. The setup does not say three *different* features. So this is actually an allowable setup:

```
1  F \
2  F  )
3  F /
4  F
5  F
```

That's one three-slot finance feature and two single-slot finance features. This is perfectly legal and it obeys all of the rules!

A lot of people are afraid to make a diagram like the one above. "Is it allowed?" they ask. Yes! On logic games, if something isn't explicitly forbidden, then it's allowed.

This game is *very* flexible. Once you internalize that, it's *easy*!

Ok, let's look at the rules. If there's no feature, there's a graphic. Simple enough.

Next the listed rules:

- Multi slot features are consecutive

This just means that if a finance feature is in three slots, then it's in 1,2,3 or 2,3,4 and not 1,3,5.

- If there's a finance or technology feature, we need one of those in slot 1.

I believe this means that if, say, there's a tech feature in slot 3, then slot 1 needs a tech or finance feature. I don't think this rule means you need the same type in slot 1.

Note also that simply having a tech or finance feature in slot 1, and nowhere else, is also legal.

- Only one industry feature

Pretty straightforward. Don't make more than one industry feature.

Marketing has no rules.

I actually drew *no* diagrams for the main setup on this game. What would I draw? The rules were so clear that it was easiest just to read them again if I forgot.

I think the main difficulty on this game is self-imposed. You probably want to think there must be more restrictions, because games tend to be restricted.

Nope. This game is incredibly open. Happens sometimes. The zones game is another example.

Main Diagram

I drew no diagram. See the setup for an explanation. In timed conditions on individual questions I made diagrams that look like this:

```
1  F ⟍
2  F  ⟩
3  F ⟋
4  F
5  F
```

Note that in these explanations I made no diagrams as none seemed necessary. But I encourage you to draw diagrams that match this style if needed. Drawing diagrams yourself can help clarify the game.

I didn't make symbols for the rules because it's very easy to remember the rules and reread the list if you forget. Plus there are no good symbols for the listed rules.

Question 19

For acceptable order questions, go through the rules and use them to eliminate answers one by one.

Rule 1 eliminates **E.** If a feature spans more than one slot, then those slots must be consecutive. Here marketing is in slots 2 and 4.

Rule 2 eliminates **B** and **C.** If there is a technology or finance feature, then the first slot must have a technology or finance feature. In **B** the first slot is a graphic, in **C** the first slot is an industry feature.

Rule 3 eliminates **A.** There can't be more than one industry feature.

D is CORRECT. It violates no rules.

Question 20

This question says there is no tech feature, and there is a finance features in slots 4 and 5.

Rule 2 says that if there's a finance feature, then a tech or finance feature must be in slot one.

Since there are no tech features in this question, the first slot must be a finance feature. **A is CORRECT.**

Question 21

As I wrote in the setup, *almost everything* is allowed in this game. This question is asking what can't be true. So don't spend too long on answers. If they don't seem impossible or affects a rule, they're probably possible. You should move on to answers more likely to be correct.

A complies with rule 3. That helps make it possible, not impossible.

B triggers rule 2, but that only means that a tech or finance feature must be in slot one. That's possible.

C is possible if we place a finance feature in slot one. And we can do that.

D works if we place a tech feature in slot one.

E is CORRECT. What **E** tells us is that there are *no* finance or tech features except in slot 5. And the question says that there *is* a feature in slot 5, so it must be finance or tech.

So this answer violates rule 3. It places a finance or tech feature in slot 5, but it doesn't place a finance or tech feature in slot 1.

Note: B, C and **D** all trigger rule two. But these answers work. We just have to put either finance or tech in slot one. Remember that rule two says we must put finance *or* tech. We don't need to place the same one that appeared elsewhere. So finance in slot 1, tech in slot 3 works, for example.

73

Question 22

This answer places an industry feature in slot 1. We know two things that are relevant:

- There are no more industry features (rule 3)
- There are no finance or tech features (rule 2)
- We need at least three features

Since we can't have industry or finance or tech features, the other two features must be marketing.

So at minimum those fill slots 2,3 or 3,4 or 4,5. Either way one of slots 2,3,4 has a marketing feature. So **D** is **CORRECT.**

A and **B** can't be true. We can't have more than one industry feature (rule 3).

C and **E** could be true, but don't have to be. Marketing could be in 4,5 or 2,4 as well.

Question 23

As I wrote in the setup, *almost everything* is allowed in this game. This EXCEPT question is effectively asking us what must be false.

So don't spend too long on answers. If the answers don't seem obviously banned, then they're probably allowed. You should move on to answers more likely to be correct.

Remember that except for industry, we can have an unlimited amount of other features. So to make the wrong answers work you just need to add two of the feature not mentioned.

A works if we also have two tech features.

B works if we also have two tech features.

C works if we also have two finance features.

D is **CORRECT.** We need at least three features. But in **D,** we have just one marketing feature, and no finance or tech features.

The only thing left is industry. But rule 3 says that we can only have one industry feature. So this answer allows two features max.

E works if we also have two finance features.

Note: Remember, rule two says that a finance *or* a tech feature fill slots one. So if, say, there's a single finance feature in slot 3, then this works as long as we have a tech feature in slot 1.

Appendix: LR Questions By Type

Strengthen

Section I, #9
Section I, #15
Section I, #21
Section III, #6
Section III, #21

Weaken

Section I, #5
Section I, #11
Section III, #13
Section III, #22

Sufficient Assumption

Section I, #23
Section III, #15

Parallel Reasoning

Section I, #25
Section III, #9

Flawed Parallel Reasoning

Section I, #22
Section III, #14

Necessary Assumption

Section I, #1
Section I, #3
Section III, #2
Section III, #17
Section III, #19
Section III, #23
Section III, #25

Method of Reasoning

Section I, #4
Section III, #11

Must Be True

None on this preptest. Am noting this because this is unusual. Most prior tests had 1-3. This test has a lot more "most strongly supported".

Most Strongly Supported

Section I, #13
Section I, #17
Section I, #20
Section III, #4
Section III, #24

Paradox

Section I, #6
Section I, #19
Section III, #5

Principle

Section I, #2
Section I, #10
Section III, #3
Section III, #12

Identify The Conclusion

Section I, #8
Section III, #8

Point At Issue

None on this preptest. Am noting this because this is unusual. Most prior tests had 1-3.

Complete the Argument

Section III, #1

Role in Argument

Section I, #14
Section I, #16
Section III, #20

Flawed Reasoning

Section I, #7
Section I, #12
Section I, #18
Section I, #24
Section III, #7
Section III, #10
Section III, #16
Section III, #18

Thank You

First of all, thank you for buying this book. Writing these explanations has been the most satisfying work I have ever done. I sincerely hope they have been helpful to you, and I wish you success on the LSAT and as a lawyer.

If you left an Amazon review, you get an extra special thank you! I truly appreciate it. You're helping others discover LSAT Hacks.

Thanks also to Anu Panil, who drew the diagrams for the logic games. Anu, thank you for making sense of the scribbles and scans I sent you. You are surely ready to master logic games after all the work you did.

Thanks to Alison Rayner, who helped me with the layout and designed the cover. If this book looks nice, she deserves credit. Alison caught many mistakes I would never have found by myself (any that remain are my own, of course).

Thanks to Ludovic Glorieux, who put up with me constantly asking him if a design change looked good or bad.

Finally, thanks to my parents, who remained broadly supportive despite me being crazy enough to leave law school to teach the LSAT. I love you guys.

About The Author

Graeme Blake lives in Montreal Canada. He first took the LSAT in June 2007, and scored a 177. It was love at first sight. He taught the LSAT for Testmasters for a couple of years before going to the University of Toronto for law school.

Upon discovering that law was not for him, Graeme began working as an independent LSAT tutor. He teaches LSAT courses in Montreal for Ivy Global and tutors students from all around the world using Skype.

He publishes a series of LSAT guides and explanations under the title LSAT Hacks. Versions of these explanations can be found at LSAT Blog, Cambridge LSAT and LSAT Hacks, as well as amazon.com.

Graeme is also the moderator of www.reddit.com/r/LSAT, Reddit's LSAT forum. He worked for a time with 7Sage LSAT.

Graeme finds it unusual to write in the third person to describe himself, but he recognizes the importance of upholding publishing traditions. He wonders if many people read about the author pages.

You can find him at http://lsathacks.com and www.reddit.com/r/LSAT.

Graeme encourages you to get in touch by email, his address is graeme@lsathacks.com. Or you can call 514-612-1526. He's happy to hear feedback or give advice.

Further Reading

I hope you liked this book. If you did, I'd be very grateful if you took two minutes to review it on amazon. People judge a book by its reviews, and if you review this book you'll help other LSAT students discover it.

Ok, so you've written a review and want to know what to do next.

The most important LSAT books are the preptests themselves. Many students think they have to read every strategy guide under the sun, but you'll learn the most simply from doing real LSAT questions and analyzing your mistakes.

At the time of writing, there are 75+ official LSATs. The most recent ones are best, but if you've got a while to study I recommend doing every test from 19 or from 29 onwards.

This series (LSAT Hacks) is a bit different from other LSAT prep books. This book is not a strategy guide.

Instead, my goal is to let you do what my own students get to do when they take lessons with me: review their work with the help of an expert.

These explanations show you a better way to approach questions, and exactly why answers are right or wrong.

If you found this book useful, here's the list of other books in the series:

(Note – the series was formerly titled "Hacking the LSAT" so the older books still have that title until I update them)

- Hacking The LSAT: Full Explanations For LSATs 29-38, Volume I
- Hacking The LSAT: Full Explanations For LSATs 29-38, Volume II
- Explanations for '10 Actual Official LSATs Volume V' – Volume I, LSATs 62-66
- Explanations for '10 Actual Official LSATs Volume V' – Volume I, LSATs 67-71
- LSAT 72 Explanations (LSAT Hacks Series)
- LSAT 73 Explanations (LSAT Hacks Series)
- LSAT 74 Explanations (LSAT Hacks Series)

Keep an eye out, as I'll be steadily publishing explanations for other LSATs.

If you *are* looking for strategy guides, try Manhattan LSAT or Powerscore. Unlike other companies, they use real LSAT questions in their books.

I've written a longer piece on LSAT books on Reddit. It includes links to the best LSAT books and preptests. If you're serious about the LSAT and want the best materials, I strongly recommend you read it:

http://redd.it/uf4uh

(this is a shortlink that takes you to the correct page)

Free LSAT Email Course

This book is just the beginning. It teaches you how to solve individual questions, but it's not designed to give you overall strategies for each section.

There's so much to learn about the LSAT. As a start, I've made a free, five day email course. Each day I'll send you an email teaching you what I know about a subject.

LSAT Email Course Overview

- Intro to the LSAT
- Logical Reasoning
- Logic Games
- Reading Comprehension
- How to study

What people say about the free LSAT course

These have been awesome. More please!!! - **Cailie**

Your emails are tremendously helpful. - **Matt**

Thanks for the tips! They were very helpful, and even make you feel like you studied a bit. Great insight and would love more! - **Haj**

Sign up for the free LSAT email course here

http://lsathacks.com/email-course/

p.s. I've had people say this free email course is more useful than an entire Kaplan course they took. It's 100% free. Good luck - Graeme

Made in the USA
Las Vegas, NV
11 February 2024

85639173R00046